A JOURNEY

OF

LITERARY AND ARCHÆOLOGICAL RESEARCH

IN

NEPAL AND NORTHERN INDIA

1. TEMPLES AND BATHING-GHATS AT THE SHRINE OF PAÇUPATI, NEPAL.

2. ISLAND-PALACE IN THE LAKE AT OODEYPORE.

Photographed by the Author.

A JOURNEY

OF

LITERARY AND ARCHÆOLOGICAL RESEARCH

IN

NEPAL AND NORTHERN INDIA

DURING THE WINTER OF 1884-5

CECIL BENDALL

ASIAN EDUCATIONAL SERVICES
NEW DELHI ★ MADRAS ★ 1991

ASIAN EDUCATIONAL SERVICES.
* C-2/15, S.D.A. NEW DELHI-110016
* 5 SRIPURAM FIRST STREET, MADRAS-600014.

Price: Rs. 195
Special Price for Nepal: Rs. 195 (N.C.)
AES Reprint: 1991
First Published: 1886 CAMBRIDGE
ISBN: 81-206-0615-9

Published by J. Jetley
for ASIAN EDUCATIONAL SERVICES
C-2/15, SDA New Delhi-110016
Processed by APEX PUBLICATION SERVICES
New Delhi-110016
Printed at Hi-tech Offset Printers
Delhi-110053

A JOURNEY

OF

LITERARY AND ARCHÆOLOGICAL

RESEARCH

IN

NEPAL AND NORTHERN INDIA,

DURING THE WINTER OF 1884–5.

BY

CECIL BENDALL, M.A.

FELLOW OF GONVILLE AND CAIUS COLLEGE, CAMBRIDGE;
PROFESSOR OF SANSKRIT IN UNIVERSITY COLLEGE, LONDON;
MEMBER OF THE ROYAL ASIATIC SOCIETY.

CAMBRIDGE:
AT THE UNIVERSITY PRESS.
1886

Cambridge:

PRINTED BY C. J. CLAY, M.A. & SON,

AT THE UNIVERSITY PRESS.

PREFATORY LETTER.

Dear Mr Vice-Chancellor,

The following pages are intended to fulfil the promise made in my letter, published by your predecessor in the *University Reporter* of 26 May 1885, of submitting to the University a detailed account of my recent tour in India, in accordance with the conditions of Grace 2 of the Senate of 19 June 1884. I then expressed a hope that the present publication might be ready early in last Michaelmas term; but circumstances rendered that impossible, and even now it is not as full as I could have wished. It seemed better however to make no further delay. The chief matters postponed are the descriptions of several interesting and little-known MSS. and the publication of several inscriptions.

In the descriptions of the new literature that I have brought to light, I fear my brief notices will seem very partial and meagre, if compared, for instance, with the admirable accounts and extracts given in the recent reports of Professors Peterson and Rāmakṛishṇa Bhāṇḍārkar. Some allowance will doubtless be made for the difference of situation between scholars working with the ever-helpful pandit always at hand in the glorious λαμπρὸς αἰθήρ of India, and the single-handed efforts of one whose hours of daylight (such as it is in a London winter) are chiefly consumed by official work. I have thus had to forego describing in detail the fine representative collection of Sanskrit and Prakrit literature purchased by me at Bombay from Pandit Bhagvān Dās, and to confine myself to reproducing his rough list without classifying the MSS., as I have done in the case of my own collection. Still less have I been able to give notes on the more remarkable works, as I have attempted in that case. An adequate description, indeed, would be the work of years rather than of months. My want of daylight leisure has also prevented me publishing all my inscriptions; but I hope to be able to deal with them before very long.

My acknowledgments of help received during the journey itself will be found at the end of Part I. In reading these, I trust my native friends will recognise their own names. At the risk of occasionally seeming pedantic, I have transliterated their names like other Indian words, without reference to local pronunciation[1].

In the preparation of the present work, I have to thank several friends, especially Professor William Wright, for many valuable hints and for kind and prompt help in revising the proofs. Professor J. G. Bühler of Vienna has likewise aided in the revision of my inscriptions. Professor Cowell, Dr Daniel Wright, Professors Weber, Jacobi, and Adams have also favoured me with ready answers to various special questions that I have ventured to address to them.

I feel it also my sad duty to refer here to not fewer than three of those who aided in my work in various ways, and have been removed by death since I commenced it.

The first is the late Raṇa-uddīpa Siṃha (Runoodeep Sing), Mahārāja (Prime Minister) of Nepal, who was slain during the disturbances in Kathmandu in November last. Whoever may be the new rulers, I trust they will be no less ready than the late Premier to afford a courteous reception to scholars.

Next I must mention Mr James Fergusson, incomparably the soundest and most accomplished critic of our day in his particular branch of art, who took a kindly interest in the journey now recorded, both before and after it was undertaken.

---

[1] As for Bengali, where the divergence of spelling and pronunciation is greatest, attempts to put them into 'popular' spelling appear often as ridiculous in the eyes of the Hindus as in our own, if we may judge from the correspondence in the "Pandit" for April 1869 (Vol. III. p. 248).

Perhaps one of the last opinions he delivered on his favourite subject of Indian art was in reference to the photograph of the temple at Oodeypore now published[1].

Lastly I have to mourn the heavy loss, still fresh in the mind of every Cambridge reader, of one of the most trusty, most energetic, and most appreciative friends and supporters of the present work, and, let me add, of the worker also. Under the auspices of Henry Bradshaw, the greatest librarian of our time, it was my privilege to commence my study of manuscripts. I shall never forget the sympathy, and even enthusiasm with which he used to follow, in the minutest palæographical and chronological details, my endeavours to arrange the great Nepal collection of our Library, nor my debt to him for many a hint and practical direction in the work of re-arranging many masses of confused leaves and in describing and registering the re-arrangement. I well remember a phrase of his, used not without a touch of irony significant for us librarians: "My favourite occupation is putting rubbish in order." Though no professed Orientalist, he had something to teach specialists in all branches. He had, as many others can testify, a very strong sense of the value of our Oriental collections, and not the least of that sent by Dr Wright from Nepal. My proposal to visit that country found in him from the first one of its most friendly and warmest supporters. I have seldom received more real encouragement than from the expression of the genial and firm support that he was pleased to give to my application to the Worts Fund on the occasion of its discussion in the Arts School on 17 June 1884.

Conscious as I am of the shortcomings of the present work, I have no keener regret in connexion with it than that it cannot be submitted to him at all events in its complete form, though some of the first part was read in manuscript by him and has been in a few places modified according to his suggestions. Yet it is some satisfaction to know his opinion of my efforts, and of their possible results and development, whether by

---

[1] See List of Illustrations, No. VII., note 2.

myself or others: and thus I feel that I cannot now do better than conclude by quoting the final sentences of the last letter of any consequence that he wrote to me,—à propos of the journey now described: "Your work is a real beginning and must lead to more good work. I only hope that you may be allowed to have a hand in it."

I remain,

dear Mr Vice-Chancellor,

Yours faithfully,

CECIL BENDALL.

To the Reverend the Vice-Chancellor
   of the University of Cambridge.

London, *March* 1886

TABLE OF CONTENTS.

LIST OF ILLUSTRATIONS.

COLLOTYPES   (Autotype Company's process).

(Except where otherwise stated, from negatives by the author.)

[1] Not described in the text : but see Dr D. Wright's History of Nepal, p. 21.

[2] The two views from Oodeypore (I. 2 and VII) are also not described in the text, but are in fact inserted by an after-thought, the first as an attempt to give some idea of the wonderfully beautiful combination of architecture and lake-scenery, so characteristic of Rajputana, in a locality still surprisingly little known. As for the temple (No. VII), almost the only notice I find of it is in Major H. H. Coïe's First Report on Ancient Monuments, p. clxxix, where he draws attention to its astonishingly late date, A.D. 1734. As the photographs illustrating this Report are not generally accessible, I publish this, though it is by no means all I could wish it to be, until a better appears. The condition of photography in India, I may here observe, is most unsatisfactory. The ordinary European firms charge for views prices that I may characterize, from knowledge of the actual cost of photography in the country, as most exorbitant. I found however one distinctly able and enterprising photographer, somewhat more moderate in charge, Lāla Dīn-dayāl, a Digambara Jain at Indore, who seems to have brought to bear on our modern art-science some of the traditional art-feeling of his sect. For the sake of those readers who are interested in Indian architecture I may mention that this photographer has a London agent, Mr Farrer of Hanway Street, W.

LITHOGRAPHS.

PART I.

ARCHÆOLOGICAL AND GENERAL REPORT.

My tour in Northern India commenced at Bombay on Oct. 22nd, 1884.

After landing I lost little time in making the acquaintance of Pandit Dr[1] Bhagvānlāl Indrajī, whose researches in Indian antiquities, chiefly published in the *Indian Antiquary*, are well known both in India and Europe. The Pandit resides near the Valkesvar shrine—a celebrated and most picturesque place of Hindu pilgrimage, situated in strange juxtaposition to the fashionable European quarter of the Malabar Hill. In his house is a large and interesting collection of coins, copperplate grants and other antiquities. Amongst other objects I may note in particular a double-headed figure covered with inscriptions in the rare and interesting Ariano-Pali character. It is much to be desired that the Pandit or some other antiquary should publish some account of this monument.

Having made no extensive study of Indian numismatics, I offer no opinion as to the exact value of the Pandit's collection of coins, which is however strongly representative of the Gupta period; but as the Pandit has probably made more extended scientific travels than any other native of India, and these

---

[1] The Pandit was presented with the honorary degree of Ph.D. by the University of Leiden, already distinguished for its Orientalism. I trust that our own Universities will some day do honour to themselves by following this example, especially if, as seems likely, some distinguished native scholars are induced to come to Europe for the Orientalists' Congress of next year.

always with an antiquarian object, it doubtless represents a great diversity of place as well as time. I have little doubt that Dr Bhagvānlāl would readily respond to requests from institutions like the University or the British Museum for copies or impressions, from which possibly exchanges of duplicates could be arranged.

My more particular purpose in seeking the acquaintance of this great scholar was to gain some advice as to my journey to Nepal. The Pandit himself spent four months in that country in the year 1880, and published some valuable and interesting inscriptions, copied by him there, in the *Indian Antiquary* (Vol. IX. pp. 160 seq., sequel in Vol. XIV. pp. 411 seq.). Following a suggestion of my friend Professor J. G. Bühler of Vienna, who had kindly written to Dr Bhagvānlāl to interest him in my journey to Nepal, I sought to induce him to accompany me thither; but after some hesitation my proposal was declined on the ground of numerous literary engagements. I may state here, however, that on my return to Bombay the Pandit expressed regret that he had not gone with me, and further added that, should I visit Nepal again, he would accompany me both to Kathmandu and to some other parts of the country, which I shall mention later on.

I cannot however speak in too warm terms of the kind and friendly way in which this eminent scholar placed at my disposal the very exceptional experience he had gained, as the only scientific traveller who had visited this secluded country unencumbered by all the restrictions placed there on Europeans. I not only profited by numerous conversations with him during my hurried stay in Bombay, but also received after my departure several letters containing valuable hints and information as to the whereabouts of objects whose existence the Pandit had ascertained without being able to publish a description of them.

In Dr Bhagvānlāl's collection are also several early MSS. from Nepal, from which I obtained some fresh dates supplementing the chronological table of the kings of Nepal occurring at pp. xii. sqq. of my Catalogue. These are given in Appendix III. below.

On leaving Bombay for the interior I made a short detour to the great cave of Kārli, certainly among the most solemn and impressive of all the temples of the world, deeply interesting as a monument alike of the stately magnificence of ancient Buddhism, and of constructive religious art, enhanced by the venerable records with which its stones are covered. After a preliminary visit to Benares I proceeded by the Tirhut State Railway to Motihāri. I passed the Nepalese frontier near Phulwaria, not without considerable annoyance from the officials, and arrived in Kathmandu[1] on November 9th.

Here I occupied the travellers' bungalow belonging to the Government of India, and during each day was entertained by the Resident, Mr C. Girdlestone, whose kind cooperation in forwarding several of the objects of my visit I desire cordially to acknowledge. The first of the few days I was enabled to spend in Nepal had to be given up to inactivity, as the Resident considered it unadvisable to visit the city, especially for the purposes of archæological search, without acquainting the Durbar with the objects of my mission. I utilized the time, however, to some extent in preliminary work for my chief object, the acquisition of MSS., by several conversations with the Residency Pandit Indrānand, the son of the late Pandit Guṇānand, one of the *collaborateurs* in the *History of Nepal* compiled by Dr Daniel Wright, and published by the University. Such success as I had in my main object was almost entirely due to the exertions of this Pandit, to whom I am also much indebted for very attentive and courteous guidance in visiting several of the more distant localities of archæological interest. I also

---

[1] I leave the spelling of this name without diacritical marks, because I do not care for such marks in geographical names where they are not absolutely necessary as guides to an intelligible pronunciation, also because there seems great doubt as to the exact form in this case. The native chroniclers seem always to use the quasi-classical form, Kāntipur; Dr Hunter's Gazetteer has 'Khatmandu (*Káthmándú*)'; another Sanskritised form (giving a real or attempted derivation) is Kāshṭhamanḍapa (see my Catalogue, p. 100); the writer of the recent history of Nepal in Bengali, a native of Nepal whom I met in his exile, writes Kātmunḍa. In any case, let me observe that the first syllable is long (a as in 'bath'), while the accent is on the second syllable.

profited much by the cordially rendered assistance of the Residency Mīr Munshi, Durgācaraṇa Miçra. The Pandit had already gained particulars as to a list of desiderata which I had forwarded to the Resident by post: he had also obtained one MS. on approval, which I ultimately purchased. See Classified List of MSS. in Part II., § XI. No. 2.

On the 12th November I made a beginning of practical archæological work by visiting some of the places in or near the town of Kathmandu in which inscriptions had been found by Pandit Bhagvānlāl in 1880.

The very first and nearest of these seemed to illustrate forcibly how desirable it is that opportunities should be taken to reproduce these documents while they still exist.

This was the short inscription of Aṃçuvarman [*Indian Antiq.* Vol. IX. (for August, 1880), No. 8], which is described as at Satdhārā near the Rānīpokhra tank. The whole masonry of the place round the spring seems quite recently to have been demolished, and heaps of brick rubbish are lying about in all directions, the whole spot as far as the tank being now included in the parade-ground. I found no trace of the inscription, so that it would seem that the Pandit was only just in time to preserve a record of it.

I next visited Lagan-ṭol, within the town, and there saw the originals of Nos. 3 and 4 of Pandit Bhagvānlāl's series, and can testify to the great accuracy of the published reproductions of these, as I examined the dates in particular with considerable care. Near the site of No. 4, at the opposite side of the temple of Jaisi, is a specimen of a class of inscription of which I found several instances in Nepal, viz., a stone at the end of a conduit in which was formerly a spout, inscribed with the date and name of donor. The present inscription is given in full in Appendix I. with facsimile. It is dated [Çrīharsha-] Saṃvat 151 (A.D. 657), and records the donation of the conduit with *certain measures* of land by a matron named Bhojamaṭi to the temple-committee of Lanjagval for their perpetual enjoyment thereof.

On November 14th I visited the famous hill of Svayambhūnāth, of which a description, together with early myths

CAITYA OF SVAYAMBHŪNĀTH.

NEPAL.

concerning it, is to be found in Dr D. Wright's work on Nepal, pp. 23, 79 sqq. I give a view, drawn from an imperfect negative of my own, of part of the great central mound, with a curious collection of smaller stūpas of slate and stone with which the courtyard is crowded. I ascertained from some of the priests of the shrine that several Sanskrit manuscripts, including a palmleaf 'Ashṭasāhasrikā,' a paper Lalitavistara and others, were preserved here. They declined, however, to exhibit them, the custom being to produce them only on special religious occasions for the adoration of the faithful. How intelligent would be the use of such books may be inferred from the circumstance that even the chief priest to whom I addressed some simple Sanskrit phrases, did not so much as attempt to answer me in the classical language—a point of honour with every decent pandit in the plains of India.

During my pilgrimage to the shrine I found remains of an early inscription on a fallen and broken lāṭ or votive pillar, now lying along the side of a well in the courtyard. It may be seen in the illustration just at the feet of the group of garlanded worshippers and others. The inscription is at present a mere fragment, as the lower part is broken, and the upper part is worn and has been partly recovered with a thinly scratched (and to me illegible) modern inscription. The character, however, of what remains is of decided Gupta type, quite distinct from the Aṃçuvarman group of the VIIth cent. A.D., as may be seen at once from the archaic forms of क, ण and other letters, which resemble typical inscriptions of the fourth and fifth centuries; so that we may fairly infer that the shrine has an antiquity of some 1400 or 1500 years—a consideration which is interesting when taken in connexion with the literature of the spot, namely the various redactions of the Svayambhū-Purāṇa, as to which it may suffice here to refer to the citations in my Catalogue of the Buddhist Sanskrit MSS. in the University Library, p. 7. Up to the present time I have not succeeded in obtaining from the few lines that are even partly legible anything of sufficiently connected interest to make it worth publishing. I also took a photograph (not now published) at the base of the great flight of steps leading up the hill, shewing a figure of Buddha between two lions of archaic character. The figures and numerous small stūpas here are surrounded by numbers of small tablets deposited by Tibetan pilgrims. Most of them bear the familiar 'om maṇi padme hūm' in the characteristic raised (not incised) letters. A living representative of these pilgrims was standing in the foreground.

In the latter part of the same day I was favoured with an interview with His Excellency the Mahārāja or prime minister of Nepal, Raṇa-uddīpa Siṃha. On the same occasion I had the pleasure of meeting General Khaḍga Shaṃsher Siṃha, who by his friendly courtesy and excellent knowledge of English was of great assistance to me on this and several other occasions. There was also present the Durbar pandit, Vācaspati, who conversed in clear and excellent Sanskrit, in which also the Mahārāja (who is evidently much interested in the classical language) occasionally joined.

I then explained my objects in visiting Nepal, briefly referring to the work recently done by myself and by others on the literature and antiquities of the country. Permission was granted to see the Durbar library and also to copy inscriptions and to photograph buildings. I also made some suggestions as to the desirability of viewing some very ancient manuscripts and other documents mentioned to me by Dr Bhagvānlāl Indrajī as in the possession of Buddhist and other religious establishments, and a promise was made that efforts should be directed towards procuring access to these, by having them brought to the Durbar or otherwise. Judging by the great trouble that was taken to show me the Mahārāja's own MSS., it may fairly be supposed that, had my stay in the country not been curtailed as it was, some of the hopes thus raised might have been realised. On the following day I visited Bodhnāth (described in Wright's *History* p. 22, with a picture[1], and the legend of its

---

[1] The place is really flat; the apparent elevation behind the mound is obviously due to a desire on the part of the Doctor's native draughtsman to get in as many buildings as he could.

foundation at p. 100). The shrine seems almost entirely kept up by Bhotiyas and Tibetans. The adjacent village abounds in small Tibetan inscriptions, mostly of very modern appearance. I took a rough copy of a single specimen of these.

On the 16th November I made my first visit to the interesting old town of Pātan, formerly called Lalitapur or Lalitapattan, only 2½ miles from Kathmandu, but long the seat of a separate monarchy[1], and at present the chief seat of the national Buddhism. A photograph is published by Hoffman of Calcutta, which gives some idea of the singularly diversified and picturesque effect of the group of temples in the great square of the old Durbar there. They appear to be mostly of the XVIth and XVIIth centuries: and from inscriptions written in Newari, and therefore not reproduced here, I gained some particulars as to the genealogies and dates of the kings of this period, which I have incorporated in the revised table of kings supplementary to that published in the introduction to my Catalogue. See Appendix III. In a street leading through a small drill-ground, eastwards from the south-east corner of this square, I discovered two inscriptions of the VIIth century, adjacent to wells called respectively Gairī-dhārā and Sun-dhārā.

The first is dated [Çrīharsha-] Samvat 82 (A.D. 688) and records the provision made by a monarch for the due worship of a divinity as well as for the repair and cleansing of the shrine. The residue (pariçesha), if any, of the grant was to be used for the feeding of 'the Pāçupatas and Brahmans.' The executive officer of the grant is a *Yuvarāj* whose name seems to be Skanda-deva. The stone is much weather-worn at the top, but many of the remains of incisions, though nearly flattened down, are fairly legible. The experience of a stone like this showed the importance of supplementing any system of estampage or other copy from contact, by photography. At the same time I have unfortunately to add that the risks of the latter process were exemplified by the fracture of the glass of my negative, which I therefore do not publish, but give in Appendix I. an autotype

---

[1] See my *Catalogue of Buddhist Sanskrit MSS.*, Introd. p. x.

reproduction of part of the *back* of my paper copy, so that the letters appear raised instead of incised as they are in fact.

The Sundhārā inscription is dated [Çrīharsha-] Saṃvat 34 (A.D. 640) and records a grant, from a king whose name is now lost, but doubtless Aṃçuvarman, of land near the village of Māṭiṅ, the assessment (*piṇḍaka*[1]) of which is to be handed over to the Pāñcālikas, elsewhere endowed both by Aṃçuvarman and his successor Jishṇugupta (Bhagvānlāl, Inscr. 7 and 10), as a permanent endowment for the repair of a building which the king had recently restored after considerable dilapidations had occurred. As to who the Pāñcālikas were, we have no certain information. Dr Bhagvānlāl in his note (26) on his 7th inscription tells us that "the word *Pāñcālika* seems to be a technical expression corresponding to the southern Pāñcakulika and the modern 'Panch'": with which we are to compare the modern temple-committees called *guṭṭhī*. In the *History of Nepal* as translated by Dr D. Wright, the term does not seem to occur, but at p. 163 we find that (many centuries after this) a town Panāvatī (now Panautī) was founded 'near the Prayāga-tīrtha of Nepal, celebrated in the Shastras, on the site where the Pancāla-des formerly stood'; while on p. 133 we are told that Aṃçuvarman, who was reigning at the date of this inscription, "went to Prayāga-tīrtha and persuaded [the deity] Prayāga Bhairava to accompany him to Nepal." May we conjecture (until further evidence is forthcoming) from these confused and mythical traditions that the Pāñ-cālikas were a band of settlers, whom Aṃçuvarman introduced from the Kanauj and Prayāg (Allahabad) districts and whom he sought to propitiate by grants of territory and general endowment ?

Near the inscription, on the opposite side of the open square in which it stands, is a small group of images in high relief with a votive inscription in verse recording that in [Nepal] Saṃvat 203, Vāṇadeva, son of a king (*bhūnātha*) Yaçodeva, erected this image in honour of the Sun-god, which had been

---

[1] See Bhagvānlāl's Inscriptions, foot-note 31.

FIGURE OF SUN-GOD WITH INSCRIPTIONS (NO. V.)

planned by his mother. Two points of interest attach to this group, of which I accordingly made a photograph, now reproduced. (1) In view of the comparative rarity of sun-worship at the present day, it is important to get a dated figure of the deity with his attendants. In illustration of this I may mention that none of the pandits to whom I showed the photograph recognised the figure without the inscription, excepting only Dr Bhagvānlāl, who tells me that he means to publish some notes, which will surely be most acceptable, on sun-cult in India. (2) Yaçodeva being unknown as a king of Nepal proper, it is reasonable to suppose that he was a neighbouring petty rāja; as such he may have been the father of the first of the new line who about this time (Wright p. 160, and Bhagvānlāl, *Ind. Ant.* Dec. 1884) took possession of the Nepalese throne. It is true that the first of this line is called Vāma-(Bāma-)deva, not Vānadeva; but such errors of a letter where the sound is similar are not uncommon in these *vaṃçāvalīs*: thus Ānanda, known to us from the MS. colophons, is always called Nanda in the chronicles; so too his successor is variously called Mitra and Amṛita. I suppose, then, Vānadeva to have been at this time (A.D. 1083) intriguing (cf. Wright, l.c.) as *yuvarāj* with the people of Patan and to have enjoyed his two years of sovereignty about three or four years later. See Appendix III.

About 20 yards up a lane leading southwards from the same square is a conduit stone with a line or two of chipped and obliterated letters of archaic type.

The next day was occupied by second visits to the inscriptions near the Jaisi temple in Kathmandu and to Svayambhūnāth hill to further the investigations summarized above.

Nov. 18, 19. After a day spent chiefly in work connected with MSS., I walked to the charmingly situated shrine of Gokarṇa, and attempted to reach from thence the hill of Chāngunārāyaṇa, but being misdirected, had to postpone the visit to another opportunity, which, I regret to state, did not occur. I have written to Nepal, however, for a copy of the missing parts of Pandit Bhagvānlāl's reproduction of the important inscription there, and venture to hope that after the general progress made in the country since the Pandit's attempt seven years ago[1], no difficulties will now be experienced in getting the whole copied.

On Nov. 20 I visited Kīrtipur, but failed to find any early inscriptions; but on my return thence through the southern part of Kathmandu I discovered a conduit inscription in a place called Varam-ṭol. It is dated [Nepal] Saṃvat 259 (A.D. 1139), by a curious coincidence the same reign and date as Add. MS. 1643, second colophon, in our University Library. The characters have a special interest as being, I think, hitherto unnoticed in inscriptions and bearing a very distinct analogy to the hooked-top written character of the period, peculiar to Nepal, as to which I may be permitted to refer to my remarks in the Palæographical Introduction to my Catalogue of MSS. from Nepal. See Appendix I.

The language of the inscription is somewhat faulty in its Sanskrit and relates to the construction of the conduit.

Nov. 21. The archæological work of the next day was chiefly in Kathmandu.

Here I took a photographic view now produced in auto-type of a portion of the great Durbar-square, often photographed from different points. I selected the Kumārī-deval at its S.W. corner as a typical Nepalese temple, showing in the background a building somewhat characteristic in style, which Dr D. Wright explains to me to be an annexe to the Durbar, used on ceremonial occasions.

Further I selected a stūpa in a court behind the houses in a narrow but busy street leading northwards from the square and called Eṭṭa-ṭol, as an example of this kind of erection still found even in the middle of the larger towns, and usually standing, as this one does, in large open squares which must be of great sanitary advantage in a place where to western notions every law of health seems reversed[2].

---

[1] See the *Indian Antiquary*, Vol. IX. 160.

[2] Dr Daniel Wright's remarks (*History of Nepal*, p. 12) are not at all too severe from a European doctor's point of view. I can only say that the con-

KUMĀRĪ-DEVAL, KATHMANDU.

KVACCHA - DEVAL, NEAR PATAN,

NEPAL.

To face p. 11.

In the vicinity I found an inscription dated [Nepal] Saṃvat 818 (A.D. 1698), reign of [Bhā]skaramalla (see Revised Table, Appendix III.).

Nov. 22.   On this day a second visit to Patan yielded some of the results anticipated in the account of the place given above, and I also took occasion to photograph the Kvaccha-deval which stands outside the town to the N.E. and near the river. From my photograph a lithographic drawing has been made, which is now published. My visit to this temple was due to a drawing (No. 21) in a series prepared some 50 years ago for Mr Brian Hodgson, at once the greatest and least thanked of all our Indian Residents, when in charge at Kathmandu.

Mr Hodgson kindly lent me the series for my journey and the present report: and has directed that it is to be hereafter deposited in the India Office Library. I observe that in the drawing in question a smaller, two-storied, temple is added to the right hand of the large one. This is stated in a foot-note to be "Sacred to Sarasvati, built by Tejnám 567, Newar era"; but there is no trace of this building now. It would be interesting to learn how it disappeared; it was certainly not pulled down to gain room, as the temple stands quite beyond the town. It occurs to me as possible that Mr Hodgson's native draughtsman, a weak point with whom was trying to get too much into a picture, inserted a temple from some other place to make a pleasing composition. If I could make a longer visit to Nepal, I should certainly try to clear up this point, as 567 (A.D. 1447) is somewhat early for such a building as that shown in the drawing.

Near the N.W. corner of the town stands the temple of

dition of an ordinary eastern town, say Cairo or Benares, gives one no idea at all of Kathmandu. The nearest thing I found in India were some terrible lanes in the native capital (in most respects so 'advanced') of Jeypore. But as the people seem stronger and far more active than most of the inhabitants of India, sanitary criticism is a little disarmed. It would be certainly a pity, and more-over useless, as Dr Wright points out, to destroy the old buildings, often so charmingly picturesque, simply to apply laws made for a less hardy race. I am bound however to add, that since I left Kathmandu, and indeed since I wrote the above lines, a very severe outbreak of cholera has occurred in the town.

Kumbheçvara (Çiva), which I have selected for illustration as a fine and hitherto unnoticed specimen of Nepalese architecture. In the extensive and picturesque courtyard of this temple are several inscriptions. The earliest is clearly and evenly cut on a slab of slate, so smooth as to allow of my making a heel-ball copy. The inscription is dated in Nep. Saṃv. 512 (A.D. 1392), and records the foundation of the temple by one Jayabhīma to promote the recovery of his wife from a fever; Çiva however took her to his heaven; but the husband kept his word, and with the consent of his second wife Abhayalakshmī and his sons, built a lofty temple (prāsāda) to Çiva Kumbheçvara with *torans* (trabeate arches), in place of the mere dwelling-house (āvāsa) which had housed the god before. He likewise cleared the ground and surrounded it by walls, subsequently adding a square-built treasury (?) (chāturmukhakoça), which, as well as the temple, he enriched with precious ornaments. I had not time to work out fully the archaeology of this fine temple, but I noted on the main building a long inscription dated 921 (A.D. 1801), apparently referring to a restoration. See the autotype reproduction of my negative.

On the outskirts of the town are the Ipi-tūda chaitya-mound and the Ipi-vihāra. The former is of simple form and preserves the wooden poles which appear in Mr Hodgson's sketch of the place[1]. To the latter, which seemed a typical and ancient vihāra, I was not allowed entrance beyond the door. In all matters of this kind I always found the adherents of Buddhism—once the most liberal of religions—more superstitious than the lowest of the Hindus and as intractable as the most bigoted of the Jains of India.

Close to the above-named temple is a building, obviously a Buddhist vihāra, to which, as it has passed into the hands of Hindus, being now a "Bhagvan-deval," I gained access, and photographed the quaint courtyard, in which may be still seen all round the latticed apartments where the reading of the law

---

[1] Dr Wright does not give this chaitya any special name. It is No. 3 in his note on p. 116 of his history.

TEMPLE OF KUMBHEÇVARA, PATAN.

Photographed by the Author.

DISUSED BUDDHIST MONASTERY, PATAN.

Photographed by the Author.

and other religious exercises were carried on. See the autotype reproduction.

On Nov. 23—24 I made a two days' visit to Bhātgāon, staying there in a house kindly placed at my disposal by H. E. the Mahārāja.

To the right of the temple of Bhairava, in one corner of the great square, I found an inscription of Yakshamalla dated N.S. 560 (A.D. 1440), of which I took a rough squeeze.

Near the celebrated brass gate of the palace I noticed an inscription of Ranajitamalla, dated N.S. 874 (A.D. 1754), the latest date of any document that I have observed previous to the Gorkha conquest.

In this town I obtained direct access to a collection of MSS., several of which were in Bengali or in Maithili character and dated in the peculiar local Lakshmana Sena Samvat (A.D. 1106). Amongst others I noted a copy of a rare grammatical commentary, the Bhāshāvṛitti by Purushottama, and portions of a work called Nyāyaçāstrasmṛiti written at Kathmandu in the VIth century of Nepal: a Newari commentary was added to the text and the work seemed similar to the 'Mānava-nyāya-çāstra' of Nārada, subsequently purchased by me at Kathmandu. In Dhruva-ṭol I found a small and fragmentary inscribed slab in the centre of a raised platform now chiefly used for threshing.

Further up the winding lane which forms the chief street of the town, in a place called Golmādhi-ṭol, I found another inscription in more perfect condition. This I have already published in the *Indian Antiquary* for 1885. As there stated, the inscription is to be compared with others of the same two rulers in the series already referred to (see the *Indian Antiquary*, Vol. IX. pp. 169 foll.) edited by Drs Bhagvānlāl and Bühler, which give the dates of Samvat 34 and 39, referred to the era of Çrīharsha and thus corresponding to A.D. 640—46. Independently of Nepalese evidence, we know from Hiuen Thsang that Amçuvarman flourished in the first half of the VIIth century A.D.; so that the date of the present inscription, 318, accords perfectly with Al-Berūnī's Gupta-Vallabhi era of A.D. 319[1], as we thus get for the inscription the date of A.D. 637, which admirably accords with what we know already of the two rulers just named. Compare now the continuation of the above-cited paper in the *Indian Antiquary*, Vol. XIII. p. 422, etc. I of course photographed this stone, and the reproduction from my negative is given with my transcript in Appendix I.

The other inscription, as far as it remains, is a duplicate of the same proclamation addressed to the same villagers, together with the inhabitants of several other districts, the boundaries of which are accurately given both by the cardinal points and by land measurements. A reproduction of a portion only of my squeeze of this inscription is given in Appendix I., and this merely on account of the dissimilarity of the *style* of character from the other. Though of course contemporaneous, the writing is freer and more sloping, and, so to say, cursive in effect.

Later on I took note of two more inscriptions: the first near the temple of Nārāyaṇa in Khaumār-ṭol, the second in a *math* or quasi-collegiate establishment, behind No. 12 Valacche-ṭol. I regret that the crowd of idle followers who pursued me into the quiet little courtyard where this inscription, with some others of later date, was fixed, so disturbed the tenants of the *math* that, on returning to take a copy, I found the door closed against me. I generally found, I may observe, that, in Nepal, where Tibetans and Chinamen attract no notice, the mere dress of a European is sufficient to draw a train of 30 or 40 idlers, which would soon be doubled if an object like a photographic camera were produced.

It may be noted in illustration of the force of Hindu customs in Nepal just as in the plains, that I observed during my walk through the town a picturesque group in a courtyard listening to a reading of the Bhāgavata-purāṇa from the lips of a demonstrative *guru*, who spoke the *çlokas* with much gesticulation and a peculiar unctuousness in the delivery of words like *Parameç-*

---

[1] See Fergusson's *Indian Architecture*, Appendix, and Oldenberg's Paper on Indian dates, translated in *Indian Antiquary*, x. (p. 268, foll.).

vara, that quite gave the effect of "the blessed word Mesopotamia." I fear there were not a dozen people in the town who could understand the Sanskrit of this work any more than the women and children who piously formed part of the congregation, and it is rather characteristic of a good deal of such religion, that the chance passer-by, who might have understood, was not allowed beyond the threshold.

My second day at Bhātgāon was partly occupied in photographing inscriptions and other objects. I also took a rough squeeze of the inscription of Yakshamalla noted above.

On this day I made some further efforts in my search for MSS., and my success was greater than I expected, but my negotiations were, I fear, interfered with by the officiousness of the Nepalese *mukhya,* or guard in attendance on me. As a general rule I had nothing to complain of in the demeanour of these men; on the contrary, on several occasions, so far from acting as spies or standing in the way of my investigations, they were of great use in overcoming the stupid prejudices against strangers manifested especially by the Buddhists of this country.

Nov. 26. After a day spent in work at MSS., with only short excursions, I made a third visit to Patan.

After photographing one of the inscriptions noted above, I explored as carefully as possible the western side of the town. Here, in a place called Puṃcaligāvāhār, I found a water-spout inscription bearing characters of the same period as those of the Mānadeva inscription noted above at p. 10. Both the dates however and the king's name are so far chipped away as to be, I fear, quite beyond recovery.

Not far from the same place I found a small tablet of slate dated N.S. 523 (A.D. 1403) and recording in Newari, mixed with Sanskrit, a religious donation "in the reign of the Yuvarāja Jayadharma-malla." In A.D. 1400 (*Catal.* Introd. p. ix. and table), we find from the colophon of our University Library MS. Add. 1664 a triple regency of Jayadharma with his two younger brothers: from this inscription it would seem that in 1403 Jayasthiti was still alive (as Jayadharma is called *yuvarāja*), but had abdicated at some time subsequent to A.D. 1392 in favour of his three sons; while subsequently the eldest superseded the other two in the regency. Finally in A.D. 1412 we find the second brother Jayajyoti[1] perhaps reigning alone. It is a curious illustration of the irregularity of the Nepalese chronicles that none of them, including that recently[2] commented on by Dr Bhagvānlāl Indrajī, make any mention of these three brothers, but agree in making Yakshamalla the son and immediate successor of Jayasthiti. Compare the revised table of kings of Nepal in Appendix III.

I proceeded next to photograph the picturesque tank known as Chāyavāhā. The Buddhist stūpa on the left bears inscriptions dated N.S. 577 and 579 (A.D. 1457—9).

The whole scene was selected as a favourable and characteristic specimen of the picturesqueness of the Nepalese town, showing as it does specimens of the tumular and pagoda styles of Nepalese religious architecture, and of the equally characteristic domestic work with carved wood fronts and overhanging eaves.

Nov. 27. On this day H. E. the Mahārāja kindly sent me a number of coins to examine. All with one exception were Nepalese silver of the XVIIth and XVIIIth centuries. I have noted a few dates and kings' names, not hitherto noticed, in my revised table of kings given below in Appendix III.

But the great event of this day was my visit to the Mahārāja's library. I did not, however, enter the room in which the books are usually kept, but the whole collection, consisting of many thousands of MSS., was brought for me from the palace to the Durbar-school building. So much trouble having been taken for my convenience, I made no enquiries as to the library room itself. Possibly the books are usually stored in one of those small rooms in which some of the best Indian collections of manuscripts (e.g. that in the splendid palace at Oodeypore)

---

[1] Catal. p. 155 ad fin.

[2] *Ind. Ant.* Dec. 1884, p. 414. In preparing this Report I have also made use of a MS. of the Vaṃçāvalī (acquired through Dr Wright by the British Museum), as far as my scanty knowledge of Hindi enabled me to verify statements from its crabbed dialect.

TANK WITH BUDDHIST CAITYA AND HINDU TEMPLE, CHĀYĀ-VAHĀ, PATAN.

Photographed by the Author.

are even now kept and which contrast so curiously with European ideas of a commodious library. If this be the case, we must hope that educational progress[1], now, we trust, commencing in Nepal, will extend to the affording of still greater and more regular facilities for the study of the unique literature of the country preserved in this collection of MSS., in many respects, as we shall see, the finest in India.

Several pandits were assembled to assist me, among them Damaruvallabha Panta, known as a scholar beyond his native country and now teacher of Sanskrit in the *pāṭhsālā*. As to the obliging library-staff, I will only say that, however the books are *kept*, they are *found* with a quickness that many a European library cannot equal. As far as I know, I am the only European who has seen this collection, but some information as to its contents has on two occasions been placed in European hands.

One of these accounts is to be found in the lists sent to the University Library by Dr D. Wright, of which an abstract is given in my catalogue at p. 17.: but I always understood that, so far from having seen the collection, he had doubts as to its existence; hence the remark there added, "It is impossible to say whether such a collection really exists," a statement which I am now glad to be able to reverse.

Another account is to be found in an official paper—like so many others, unknown to the few whom it might really benefit —kindly unearthed for my enlightenment by Mr A. Mackenzie, Home Secretary to the Government of India, at his office in Calcutta, during my subsequent visit to that place. It bears the somewhat strange title: "List of Sanskrit Works supposed by the Nepalese Pandits to be rare in the Nepalese Libraries at Khatmandoo." At the end occurs the subscription:

"R. Lawrence, Resident, Nepal Residency.
The 2nd of August, 1868."

[1] The very existence of the building in which I saw the books is a proof of this. Ten years ago (1875) Dr Wright wrote, "The subject of schools and colleges in Nepal may be treated as briefly as that of snakes in Ireland—there are none." Now we have at least one building in which both English and Sanskrit are taught, and, as I have every reason to believe, well taught.

That both this and Dr Wright's lists refer to the real collection seen by me, was proved by the classes of literature, which correspond exactly, in name and in number of books, with the rough but classified list of books which was first placed at my service at this visit to the library. There have been, however, very numerous accessions: nor can the rough list be anything like complete, for the MSS. in the library are counted not by hundreds merely, but by thousands.

I may add that I mentioned to H.E. the Mahārāja, a possible application for copies of works in the library, and found from the pandits in charge that the services of a copyist could be readily secured. I trust therefore that efforts will be made to obtain copies of some of the rare works which I now proceed to mention.

In Grammar (*vyākaraṇa*) :

Library No.   Page in Law-
                rence's list.

1558   9   *Cāndravyākaraṇa*, with commentary by Dharma-
                    dāsa.   Palm-leaf; 159 leaves, 20 inches by 2 ;
                    straight-topped character of XII.—XIII. cent.,
                    comparable to that of Add. 1648.

It would be of especial value to our library to obtain a copy of this fine MS., as we possess the only fragments of this grammar known to exist in Europe. My present acquisitions have all but completed the text, while we have several fragments of unidentified commentaries, which this MS. would put us in the way of assigning to their authors.

Library No.   Page in list.

424   ...   *Bhāshāvṛitti*, by Purushottama, with commentary
                    called Bhāshāvṛittipañjikā by Viçvarūpa. Palm-
                    leaf, Bengali writing.

I have remarked above, p. 13, on the rarity of the text. This commentary is, I believe, quite unknown.

I next give a list of plays, of which the first only appears in Lawrence's list :

1.   Amṛitodaya nāṭaka.

2. Bhairavānanda, by Maṇika, produced under Rāja Jayasthiti (A.D. 1385—92). Compare our MS. Add. 1658 (Catal. p. 159).

3. Malayagandhinī.

4. Vidyātilaka.

5. Vimrālapana (?).

6. Çrīkhaṇḍacaritra.

None of these plays have been met with in India. I had unfortunately no time to examine them and to find how many were, like No. 2, local productions.

In *Jyotisha* (astronomy and astrology) I took notes of what seemed to me new, chiefly on behalf of Dr Thibaut of Benares, who is doing important work in this branch of literature. On my return to Benares I found that most of the works I had noted were unknown to him and to his accomplished astronomical pandit, Sudhākara Dube, of whom I shall speak later on. I may add that, though I can pretend to no special knowledge of the subject, so as to sift astronomical wheat from astrological chaff, I believe the works whose titles I subjoin to be of considerable rarity.

Library No.	Page in Lawrence.	
1459	11 also 3	Adbhutadarpaṇa.
1215	...	Jayacārya, by Narapati, with commentary (Jayalakshmī). Extracts from text only at Oxford (*Aufr. Cat.* 399 *b*).
1202	...	Mahāsaṅgrāmaratnakaraṇḍaka.
1196	...	Jayalakshmīsūryodaya. An old copy.
293	...	Saṃhitāvṛiti, by Meghapāla, 410 leaves.
1572	10	Nakshatramālā, by Jaganmohana.

Besides, I noted copies of the Rājamārtanda-jyotishapañjikā (No. 1210) and the Vasantarāja (No. 1011, an old copy) and the Horāsaṅkhyā (No. 1169), a part of the Toḍarānanda· of Toḍaramalla. See Lawrence, p. 11, where also occur the titles of several other rare works. The collection having been formed, as I was told, by the late Sir Jung Bahādur, and thus probably collected by Hindu pandits, it was not to be expected that a large number of Buddhist works would be included; none

2—2

indeed are mentioned in Lawrence's list; there is however a small number, and amongst them the following.

Library
number.

772 Abhisamayālaṅkāra, a commentary on the Prajñāpāra-mitā, by Haricandra, 158 leaves, with 7 lines on a page, in the characteristic hooked character. Doubtless the same as the commentary at Calcutta. See Rājendralāl Mitra's Nepalese Buddhist Literature, p. 194, line 12.

This is a most important work, and a copy should certainly be asked for.

1103 Lokācārasaṅgraha. A collection of ritual books with Newari translation : paper, about 50 leaves.

772 (?) Bodhicaryāvatāra, followed by another work, 50 leaves, 12 × 2 inches, various Nepalese hands, XIII—XIVth cent·

My opportunity of examining this fine collection was only for the tantalising space of about four hours, for on the following day, when by this time I was just getting my arrangements for the acquisition of MSS. into good working order, I was obliged, owing to an intimation from the Resident given some days before, to leave the Government bungalow, which I had been occupying during my stay. The reason of this was an official visit from an officer of the Public Works Department. I regret extremely, on my own account and for those interested in my journey, that this circumstance should have put an abrupt end to my visit. Had I been fully aware of the conditions under which I resided in Nepal, I should have made negotiations (and these would have been, as I infer from subsequent experience, of a simple kind) for permission to occupy the tenement for a much longer time. As it was, I had no alternative but to leave the country[1]

---

[1] Mr Girdlestone had kindly arranged with the Durbar for a permit to visit two towns in the Tarai, both unknown to scientific travel; but the want of a pandit or native agent to accompany me decided me not to avail myself of this privilege. Should I be enabled to visit Nepal again, I have little doubt the pass could be renewed, and I should then make a point of securing the assistance of some person like my friend Pandit Bhagvānlāl. Is it too much to hope that the government of Nepal may some day see their way to do something in the cause of archæological research in their country, so rich in records of the past? We note with satisfaction that several of the more enlightened native states, like

I believe it will be seen from the foregoing pages that I found sufficient archæological work to keep me busily occupied during my brief stay. My collection of Buddhist and other MSS. acquired in Nepal more than realises my own expectations of the probable success of even a much longer stay.

The architectural studies which I had proposed to myself were almost entirely precluded by want of time. I had as a rule barely time to put down my notes of dates, etc., and on no occasion could I feel that time permitted the taking of measurements and accurate observation of details, to which Mr Fergusson refers in his work on Indian Architecture (p. 299 sqq.) as a great desideratum for the proper study of this interesting chapter of Oriental art-history.

After several days' uneventful journey I reached Calcutta, where my work was much helped by the friendly and scholarly kindness of Dr Hörnle and of Mr C. H. Tawney, formerly Fellow of Trinity College, to whom indeed, as already intimated in my preliminary Report, I am also indebted for help elsewhere in India.

Here no MSS. are to be had (so far as I know), except perhaps a few modern works from Orissa, of which I have brought one specimen. This is merely a Bhāgavata-purāṇa, which the owner, Mr L. J. K. Brace, Assistant Curator of the Botanical Gardens, desired me to present to the British Museum, in connection with certain botanical specimens of which I proceed to speak.

I visited the Botanic Garden of Calcutta—the most beautiful of the kind I ever saw—mainly to obtain dried specimens for the University Library of the various kinds of palm-leaf used for writing purposes, and these the same gentleman has kindly sent, and they are deposited in the library accordingly. I had never succeeded in obtaining very definite information on

Jeypore, have engaged in such work: and it is clear from the events at the great Rāwal-pindi durbar this year that Nepal no longer desires to pursue a policy of entire isolation from the current of civilization in India generally. I need hardly add that I should always be most willing and ready to avail myself of any practicable opportunity of personally directing or in any way furthering any scheme towards this end.

this point from botanical friends at home, but Pandit Umeça-candra Çarma, the courteous librarian of the Sanskrit College, Calcutta, pointed out to me that many of the best MSS. were written, not on the leaf of the common talipot palm (tālapattra), (Borassus flabelliformis), but on the more finely grained leaf of the *teret* (Corypha taliera and C. elata).

In the Calcutta Museum, the archæological part of which has recently been admirably arranged and catalogued by the Curator, Dr Anderson, I took copies of many of the unpublished inscriptions; but I understand that they will shortly be dealt with by Mr J. F. Fleet in his forthcoming volume on Gupta inscriptions.

As to the specimen of a hitherto unnoticed character, coinciding with the writing of a unique MS. fragment brought by me from Nepal, I may refer to my notes in Part II. § 2 below (Cāndravyākaraṇa). These are given in anticipation of a fuller study of this character, which I propose to publish hereafter, since, as far as I can judge at present, this discovery seems to be among the most interesting of my journey.

In the library of the Asiatic Society I examined the colophon of the oldest of the MSS. sent from Nepal by Mr Hodgson. As mentioned in one of the reviews (*Athenæum*, Jan. 5, 1884) of the Society's recently published catalogue of this collection, entitled *Nepalese Buddhist Literature*, some misapprehension seemed to exist as to the date of this MS. The results of my reading are given in Appendix III., in my supplemental table of kings of Nepal, where the date and king's name well accord with chronological results already established.

I also took advantage of my stay in Calcutta to read some portions of Sanskrit philosophical works, the full meaning of which is rarely understood by European scholars unless they have had the advantage of instruction derived directly or indirectly from the traditional school of interpretation in India. In this matter and in many others I have to acknowledge the very kind help of Professor Maheçacandra Nyāyaratna, Principal of the Government Sanskrit College. I was very glad to be able to call myself his *praçishya* (pupil's pupil). Perhaps in this iron age the *parampará* (spiritual succession) can be passed on even through and to *mlecchas*; at any rate the best of brahmans could not have received kinder attention than I from the Professor and his pupil and assistant lecturer, Raghunāth Çāstri.

To the same friend and to another of his pupils, Bābū Haraprasāda Vandyopādhyāya, I am indebted for a most interesting afternoon spent in visiting two native schools for Sanskrit. A similar visit had been made two years before by Professor J. Jolly of Würzburg, who records his experiences most graphically in the *Deutsche Rundschau* for 1884 [1]. The first of these schools is picturesquely situated on the Hooghly bank above Calcutta at Shamnagar. The building was given by the liberal Tagore (Thākur) family, and, in spite of the doubtless sanctifying influence of *lingas* and shrines, shows, I regret to say, distinctly European influence in style.

Within, however, all is Oriental: not a chair in the place, except some kindly kept (I presume) for the infirmity of European visitors: teachers on the cushions surrounded by knots of pupils. In the highest class—that of the Nyāya philosophy—I found pupils of ages from fourteen to forty, some coming from distant parts of India. At the instance of Prof. Maheçacandra they had a disputation, much like one of our old Cambridge " Wrangles ", in which was established, for my edification, after the rules of this philosophy, the existence of God.

To the next place, Bhātpāra, I was conducted by Bābū Haraprasāda, a collaborateur in Dr Rājendralāla Mitra's *Nepalese Buddhist Literature*, and met there by Bābū Hrishikeça, both of them representatives of the few remaining old Bengali families who have for generations taken pride in endowing these simple seats of learning. It would be well, I think, for some disbelievers in Hindu disinterestedness, if they could see this body of venerable teachers, living in simple, dignified poverty, feeding as well as teaching their poorer pupils. How much in fact *is* known about such institutions by our Anglo-Indian friends, often so ready to generalize about the character of "the natives," may be estimated from the circumstance, that, though the place

[1] Bd. VII. of the *Halbmonatshefte*.

is only a few miles from the metropolis, I was (so I heard) only the third European who had ever visited it.

After a Christmas most pleasantly spent with Mr G. A. Grierson, joint compiler with my last host at Calcutta, Dr Hörnle, of the great work of a scientific Bihāri dictionary, I passed on to Benares.

On ground so well-trodden it might scarcely have been expected that any fresh archaeological discoveries would fall to my lot. Yet in a garden near the Raj Ghat I found a fragment of 10 lines in a character not later than the XIth century. As the stone was presented to me, I shall be able, when I have had leisure to examine it more carefully, to offer this, my single specimen of an original and not a mere copy of an inscription, to one of our University Museums.

The chief results of this second visit to Benares are to be found in my list of MSS. in Part II.

I also made some enquiries as to the Jain community of Benares. Owing to the kind introduction of the Raja Çiva-prasāda C.S.I., himself a member of an old Jain family, I obtained access to the printing-press, and also to the library, connected with the Mandir, or Jain temple. The Maṇḍalācārya kindly had a transcript made, for my use, of his list of MSS., adding a promise to allow copies to be taken. This transcript I give in Appendix II., merely transliterating it and correcting a few obvious slips, but without attempting to verify the exact form of each title.

This library, not previously, I believe, visited by any European, may prove critically important to editors of Jain texts, as Jain MSS. are, as a rule, obtained from Western India. Though the community is of the Çvetāmbar sect, the library contains Digambar works also, e.g. the Kathākoça[1], of which I negotiated for a copy. This arrived in England shortly after I did.

---

[1] As there appear to be several collections of Jain tales with this general title, I may explain that the work referred to is that commencing with the story of Dhanada. Two tales from it have been printed by Prof. Nīlamaṇi Nyāyālaṅkāra in his Sāhityaparicaya from the Calcutta Sanskrit College MS., on which document the editor has, in more senses than one, 'left his mark.'

At the invitation of my friend Pandit Ḍhunḍhirāja Dharm-ādhikārī I attended a committee meeting of the new library started by the pandits of Benares, chiefly, I understand, at the suggestion of the pandit just named, in memory of the distinguished scholar Bāla Çāstrī, and called Bāla Sarasvatī-bhavana. The great feature of this library is that it is a place of deposit for MSS. on loan, not necessarily for good and all. If the very numerous owners of MSS. in the city can be induced only to deposit their books there, many of the characteristic risks incidental to their preservation in Indian houses will be avoided, and many rare books will doubtless come to light. At the same time, pandits are encouraged to bequeath works to the institution.

At the meeting[1] that I attended a scheme was also started for making search as to the contents of the private libraries of the city. It is indeed satisfactory, when one hears of difficulties placed in the way of the various Government officers in their search for MSS., to find here a body of native scholars willing not only to make known their own treasures, but to assist voluntarily and unofficially in the great work of literary search. One practical advantage of the institution to European scholars is, that it affords an opportunity of getting accurately made copies of almost any of the numerous works used by the pandits of Benares. Editors of philosophical texts especially may thus at once encourage a good institution and get an accurate copy by applying here.

As to the Government College Library, its present condition under Dr Thibaut and Pandit Sudhākar seems most flourishing. MSS. are constantly added, as far as the limited funds allowed by Government permit. It is however extremely unsatisfactory and discreditable to Benares to find that many of the works registered in Dr F. Hall's *Bibliographical Index* as belonging to this library 27 years ago are not now forthcoming.

A circumstance of this kind, occurring in the metropolis of

---

[1] I subsequently found an account of this meeting given in the Kavivacana-sudhā, a Hindi journal of Benares for January 19th, 1885. My remarks on the occasion occupy a very unmeritedly large space, I fear, in the report.

Hindu learning and religion, ought to be borne in mind by all impartial persons in considering remarks like those of Dr Peterson at the end of his first Report on Sanskrit MSS. (1882—3, p. 72), directed against the sending of Sanskrit MSS. to Europe[1].

I had little time to spend in examination of the MSS. of the library, but amongst the philosophical books I noted the following as supplying information supplementary to that given by Hall.

(1) Two palm-leaf copies of the Nyāyalīlāvatī-prakāça, written in Upper Bengal in the years of the Lakshmana era 389 and 395 (A.D. 1496 and 1501) respectively.

(2) The Nyāyavācaspati, a work of which I have not found any mention in Hall, or in any other work of reference, unless it be, as Prof. Cowell has suggested to me, the Nyāya-vārttika-tātparya-ṭīkā (Hall, 21). Palm-leaf, Çaka 1531 (A.D. 1609).

(3) Kaṇādarahasya, an old copy acquired since Dr Hall's time.

(4) Praçastapadavācya (? °bhāshya), Çaka 1530 (A.D. 1608).

I trust that before long we may get a good catalogue of this important library, so that the world may be enlightened as to

---

[1] Dr Peterson will, I know, pardon me for adding a few words in self-defence as a collector for European libraries.

It seems to me that, without appealing to any national prejudices, which are out of place in questions of scholarship, a book is best kept wherever it is most safely and, in all senses, liberally kept.

As for the *safety* of MSS., every collector has his tale to tell of fine books packed away in roofs of houses, etc., and preyed on by damp and insects or other vermin. At all events the white ant has not yet been imported into our libraries.

As for *liberality in arrangement and description*, let me point out that, in spite of their advantages in respect of learned and helpful pandits, scholars in India, excepting Dr Rājendralāl Mitra and the late Dr Burnell, have given us nothing worthy of the name of a Catalogue.

Lastly as to *liberality in lending*, some Indian readers might well suppose in reading the above-cited passage that "sending to Europe" meant never coming back. Yet I am glad to be able to say that, while yet in India, I was the means of a well-known native Sanskritist's applying for and receiving a very ancient and valuable Sanskrit MS. from an English library.

the gains under the present excellent *régime*, as well as the losses since the appearance of Dr Hall's notes, which form so excellent a basis for the philosophical portion of such a compilation.

Besides much assistance generously rendered by Pandit Dhundhirāja, I received help in various ways from Dr Thibaut and Mr Venis of the Government College; also from Pandit Vindhyeçvarīprasāda, whose knowledge of bibliography is exceptionally wide; and from Pandits Lakshmīnārāyaṇa Kavi and Sudhākara Dube. The last named, who is the present librarian of the college, presented me with copies of several of his astronomical and mathematical works, written in Sanskrit. I am unfortunately not able to give an opinion on the scientific value of these, but I have deposited them in the University Library in the hope that they may be noticed, as I am informed by Dr Thibaut that Pandit Sudhākara is a mathematician of considerable originality, and that his researches deserve far more recognition than they have received, owing to his want of command of literary English. Dr Thibaut adds that he is willing to translate into English original papers by this pandit for reading before any suitable scientific society in Europe.

After some memorable days spent in Agra and its neighbourhood, I passed on to Jeypore.

Here I visited the very interesting library of H. H. the Mahārāja several times, permission—quite exceptional I believe in the absence of the prince—being most kindly granted me to visit it as often as I required. Some particulars as to this fine collection are to be found in Dr Peterson's first Report (1882—83). Much information will doubtless soon be at the disposal of scholars, as the work of cataloguing the collection is proceeding under the skilled hands of Lakshmīnātha Çāstri of Benares, assisted by Krishṇa Çāstri. Both of these pandits gave the most cordial help in my work at the library, and have been, I may add, in friendly communication with me since my return. In anticipation, I give a few notes on works that seem to be unique or otherwise remarkable. Under the subdivision of Rāmānuja philosophy, a school not much represented in libraries owing to its peculiar views as to the promulgation of its tenets, I found the following works.

Library marks.

1. *Vedārthasaṅgraha* by Rāmānuja, a MS. of 37 leaves; rare, but known to Hall, and quite recently printed at Madras in the Telugu character.

Darçana 942 and 3

2. A commentary on the preceding called *Vedārthasaṅgrahatātparya-dīpikā* by Sudarçana Sūri, who is known as a commentator on Rāmānuja's Çrībhāshya. The present commentary has, I believe, not been hitherto met with.

3. *Tattvamuktākalāpa* by Venkaṭācārya, sometimes called Venkaṭanātha. Can this be the work cited in the Sarvadarçana-saṅgraha (see Cowell and Gough's translation, p. 86, note)?

In *Jyotisha* I noted :

Jyotish 45.3

4. *Rājamṛigāṅka* by Bhojadeva, a personage to whom several works in various branches of literature are attributed. This copy was made in Çaka 1450 (A. D. 1528) by Jyotirvid Çrīdatta son of Saṅka. (?) आत्म-पठनार्थं

In dramatic literature I noted a couple of local productions:

Kāvya 36.15

5. *Janakīrāghava-nāṭaka*, attributed to the *Yuvarāj* Rāmasiṃha, son of Jayasiṃha, who was reigning about A.D. 1625. MS. written A.D. 1664.

Kāvya 37.13

6. *Prabhāvalī*, a play in four acts, composed by Harijīvana Miçra at the command of the said Rāmasiṃha when *rāja*.

I may also mention :

37.8

7. *Hāsāmṛita*, a farce composed by Vitthalakṛishṇa Vidyāvāgīça at the command of Sujanasiṃha, described as reigning in Bandelkhand ; 16 leaves.

8. *Pārthaparākrama*, a *vyāyoga* in about 500 *çlokas*, by a *yuvarāj* called Prahlāda. This is followed by the beginning of a play called

9. *Dūtāṅgada* by Rāmachandra.

I noted next two pandits' plays, written on the model of the Prabodhacandrodaya, and intended to illustrate philosophy:

Kāvya 37.5 10. *Svanubhūti-nāṭaka* by Ananta Paṇḍita son of Tryambaka.   Various schools are discussed.   63 leaves.

37.1 11. *Krishnabhakticandrikā* by Anantadeva, author of the Smritikaustubha, who flourished at the beginning of the xviith cent.

12. *Ghritakulyā*, a farce in about 250 çlokas.   MS. dated V. S. 1731 (A.D. 1674).

The above with the exception of No. 11 (as to which see Bühler, Cat. MSS. in Gujarat II. 116) are, I believe, unknown.

I noted also two copies of the

37.6
59.2 13. · *Laṭakamelana* by Çaṅkhadhara, a farce apparently satirising the Digambara Jains, who however speak ordinary dramatic Prākṛit.   Dr Bühler (*Cat. Guj*. II. 122), and also Dr Peterson in his second Report (for 1883—4) note copies of this.

I visited of course, as all travellers do, the ruined city of Amber, the former capital of the state.   At a place so much in the track of visitors I scarcely expected to find anything of fresh archæological interest, but it is a characteristic proof of the amount of quite elementary work still remaining to be done in Indian Archæology, that, in a small, though not ruined, Temple of the Sun overlooking the town I found a short inscription bearing a date nearly half a century earlier than anything hitherto known in connexion with the place.   See Appendix I.

I will add here a suggestion made by my kind host Dr T. M. Hendley, who was my guide on this occasion, that the fine 'Jagatsohana' temple in this ruined town might give many most useful hints to the architects of Christian churches in India. Indeed not only the main buildings, but the whole precincts present a strong and curious analogy to an ecclesiastico-collegiate establishment.

According to my custom of visiting schools where Sanskrit is still taught on the traditional plan, I went to H. H. the Mahārāja's Sanskrit *Pāṭhsālā*, where I was kindly received and shown round by Pandits Rāmbhaja and Çivarām.   Everything, as far as one can judge, seems progressing favourably on the old lines.

During my stay at Jeypore, I had the pleasure of many interviews with Pandit Durgāprasāda, whose knowledge and appreciation of literature are most exceptionally wide.

I next spent a day or two at Ajmere, where I copied the large XIIth century Sanskrit inscription carefully preserved in the famous Aṛhāī-din-ka Jhopra. Strangely enough, it seems to be still unpublished.

Hence I passed on to Nimbahera, whence Col. Walter, Resident at Oodeypore, had kindly arranged a *ḍāk* for me to Oodeypore.

In this city, in situation the most beautiful[1] perhaps in India, I spent a short time, without however achieving any of the success in the matter of MSS. gained by Dr Peterson some years before. I attribute this to my want of an agent. Dr Peterson had sent on his native assistants previously, and they no doubt materially prepared the way for him. Should I visit India again, I should make a point of securing the services of some pandit to assist me in this way.

In archæology, however, I found at Oodeypore many matters of interest; and here I was most materially helped by Bābū Çyāmal Dās, Kavirāj (court poet or herald) to H. H. the Mahārāṇa. My courteous host Col. Walter had kindly informed him of my approaching visit and its purposes, and the Kavirāj lost no time in extending to me the right hand of fellowship.

I proceed to give a short account of the literary work, a very important one in my opinion, on which the Kavirāj is engaged. The chief families of Rajputana have usually employed a herald or family bard, who has in some sort chronicled their deeds. Bābū Çyāmal Dās has made a most fitting use of his position as royal herald in causing these to be collected and having digests made of their contents. From these, and from the general chronicles and royal *vamçāvalīs*, which are extant for the state of Oodeypore (or Meywar), the

---

[1] See the glowing, yet not too enthusiastic description in L. Rousselet's "*L'Inde des Rajahs*" (p. 174), and the still more eloquent words of Dr Peterson (First Report, pp. 48—50), embodied in one of those footnotes which I have also supposed the strictly literary traveller may sometimes allow himself.

TEMPLE NEAR THE PALACE, OODEYPORE.
Photographed by the Author.

Kavirāj is compiling a history of this state. I was much surprised to find in his library a very fine collection of books in all the chief European languages, bearing on the history and topography of Rajputana. Bearing in mind, however, how much history and panegyric run into one another in Eastern literature, it is most important to find that, supplementing his work, is a systematically collected series of inscriptions, which exist in such numbers in these parts. The growing interest (though still it is surprisingly small) felt by native scholars in their own ancient monuments and the records they bear, is one of the encouraging sides of the influence of Western thought in India, though one must confess that Europeans may still do much to make up for the influences, so deteriorating in many ways, which they and their civilization have brought to bear on native morality and native art.

But to resume. By the direction of my kind friend I was guided to several spots interesting both for architecture and inscriptions. My guide was Pandit Rāmpratāp, who has worked specially for the inscription section of the forthcoming history. The pandit is in the employment of the Durbar, and his services both here and later at Chittor were kindly placed at my disposal by H. H. the Maharāṇa, with whom I had more than one interview, at which he manifested a most friendly interest in the objects of my visit.

I visited of course the celebrated royal cemetery, the Mahāsatī, as to which Mr Fergusson[1] remarks: "All [the tombs] are crowned by domes and all make more or less pretensions to architectural beauty; while as they are grouped together as accident dictated and interspersed with noble trees, it would be difficult to point to a more beautiful cemetery anywhere." Possibly the place has been somewhat neglected since Mr Fergusson wrote; at present the beautiful and varied effect of the architecture is seriously marred by the weeds and undergrowth, and by the want of suitable paths. Outside the precincts of the cemetery proper I was shewn by the pandit several smaller tombs, which he told me were those of ministers

---

[1] *History of Indian Architecture*, p. 471.

of the state. Several of these are evidently of considerable age and merit attention.

Not far from this is the village of Ar or Ahar, abounding in objects of archæological interest, which have never been properly described. There are several Jain temples, not all of them at present in use. In one I noted an interesting series of shrines built round the square lower end of a temple courtyard. These were later additions and in almost every case bore the name of the donor and date of erection, the dates being mostly of the XIVth century. Some of the images contained in them, however, if not the buildings themselves, were of earlier date. I noted one fine undraped figure of a Tīrthaṃkara or Jain 'apostle' bearing date [Vikrama] Saṃvat 1031 (A. D. 974). Just outside one corner of the temple wall and on a lower level, so as to be partially excavated, were cells in which the monks formerly resided. Many of these have short inscriptions in Prākṛit, and bear dates chiefly of the XVIth century of the Vikrama era.

Besides the Jain temples we find in Ar traces of forms of cult a little removed from the ordinary run of Hindu temple worship. In a temple close by that just described I noted a shrine of a Nāga or serpent, which I think is of somewhat rare occurrence in modern India. The image was four or five feet high and was erected in the XVIIth century.

The next record is that of sun-worship, comparatively rare, as already observed, and little studied or scientifically understood in India. I found here no temple of the sun, as at Amber (p. 29), but a fragment of an inscription, from which it would appear that in the reign of Çaktikumāra (X—XIth cent.) the previously existing practice of offering each year 14 *drammas* (δραχμαί) of some oblation to the sun was formally confirmed. This inscription may serve as another instance of the large amount of archæological work still to be done in India. I discovered it on a piece of marble built into some steps leading to the terrace where stands the Jain temple just described. Here it had escaped the notice of my excellent guide Pandit Rāmpratāp, though he was evidently familiar with these little visited temples and their inscriptions.

The Pandit has sent me quite recently, too late indeed for me to publish it, as he kindly desired, in the present work, a beautifully executed squeeze and transcript of another inscription discovered by him since my visit in the same locality and containing mention of the same king.

The fine Sanskrit library of the palace, where I was most kindly received by my friend the Kavirāj and a number of pandits assembled in my honour, calls for no description from me, as Dr Peterson's "Detailed Report for 1882—83," an extra number of the Bombay Asiatic Society's Journal, is in the hands of all scholars. In the library catalogue, which will, I trust, during the present reign be amplified and ultimately printed, I noted a small work of a few lines only on a strange subdivision of Çilpa-çāstra, the construction of beds, certainly very late, as the (xvth century) Vāstu-maṇḍana is quoted. It seemed to me of some interest to find an addition to this division of literature (constructive art), always so thinly represented in Indian libraries, composed at so late a date in the classical language, and a copy was kindly presented to me, which I keep as a souvenir of my visit and also to help in affording material for studies in this little-studied branch of literature, which I hope to prosecute when I have leisure.

I was now permitted to visit the ruins of the ancient city-fortress of Chittor in the same state, the scene and often the very centre of Rājpūt and Musulman warfare for so many centuries. Here again I profited by the excellent guidance of Pandit Rāmpratāp, who had spent three months on the spot copying the very numerous inscriptions bearing on Rājpūt history, and doubtless also searching for fresh ones under the piles of ruins on every side.

I observed with regret that the tree noticed by Major H. H. Cole in his first *Report on Ancient Monuments* (p. clxxxii), as growing on the top of the older of the towers of Victory, was still unremoved. Not far from the famous tower of Khumbo Rāṇa, and above the tank called by Major Cole the *gau mukh*, is a cave, which has apparently been used as a Jain hermitage. In it are several Prākrit inscriptions, in characters that appear to be of about the xivth century. I have copies of several, and should they turn out interesting I shall publish them before long. To have made a detailed study of them just now would, with the unfortunately very limited amount of *daylight* leisure at my command, have delayed the present publication too long.

My stay in Chittor was limited to a part of a day, and I could not but feel with some regret what a field for historical, archæological and artistic discovery I was leaving in the state of Meywar, both here and nearer the capital. It is certainly strange that more work of this kind has not been done hereabouts. The Government of India, which has of late manifested practical interest in archæological research, certainly seems hitherto to have been rarely successful in gaining the services of officers at once qualified to criticize the artistic and constructive details of ancient buildings and to interpret and digest the documentary evidence, both literary and monumental, connected with them.

Passing hence to Indore, I endeavoured, in this instance without success, to prosecute my work of collecting MSS. A short visit to the ancient city of Ujjain, or rather to the very modern representative of the old city, proved also unavailing. So far from finding traces of the ancient astronomical learning for which the town was once renowned, I found the pandits scarcely conversant, it would seem, even with the names of the chief works on the subject.

As my allotted time of absence was now drawing to a close, I returned to Bombay, where I met by appointment Pandit Bhagvān Dās, who has long been the energetic agent of the Bombay Government for the collection of Sanskrit MSS. By a minute of this Government the agent is allowed to sell duplicates of works in the Government collections for the use of certain institutions in this country, of which our University Library is one. A rough list of the fine collection that I purchased from him is given in Part II. § 1.

I left Bombay for Europe on March 1st.

Thus terminated a tour which, if it has not resulted in any

literary or archæological discoveries of first-rate importance,—such as can only be reasonably looked for in the work of travellers of greater experience and leisure,—may nevertheless, I believe, be held to have justified the grounds of my application to the University in respect of the Worts Fund.

There now only remains to me the pleasing duty of acknowledging the sympathy and assistance I have received from various quarters. In referring first, as becomes me in the present work, to the liberality of the University, as manifested in the grant from the fund just named, I wish particularly to testify to the great encouragement I received not only from the benefaction itself, but from the generous conditions under which it was bestowed. The only condition in fact was the preparation of a Report,—a provision which the present work is designed to fulfil; and in view of the friendly and unsparing way in which the Syndics of our University Press have met my wishes as to its publication, I may say that this very condition has been turned into an additional privilege.

I venture thus to call attention to the circumstances under which I worked for the University, not because I would imply that to those acquainted with the history of the English Universities such treatment will seem at all exceptional, but because I feel bound to bear witness, which many fellow-workers can confirm, to the great stimulus to exertion afforded by such frank confidence, unhampered by the cramping restrictions by which scholarship amongst us, when encouraged at all, is too often hindered.

My project of travelling so many thousands of miles, and buying everything of literary value to me on my way, which seemed a somewhat ambitious one, was also encouraged and furthered by the very kind and timely assistance of two friends, Professor Cowell and the Reverend A. J. Harvey, M.A., of St. James's, Paddington.

Owing to the great kindness and hospitality of the residents in almost every part of India that I visited, my journey was unexpectedly attended with so little expense that I had no occasion to avail myself of the funds lent by these friends for the purchase of MSS., but my obligation, and indirectly I may perhaps add, that of the University, is none the less.

The names of many friends and fellow-scholars in India, who so kindly entertained and in every way assisted me, will have been met with in the foregoing pages; nor would it have been so necessary to dwell on their kindness but for the recent publication of the rather crude 'ideas' of an English traveller, which I found had produced a most unpleasant effect upon the various societies that had done their best to receive him cordially; and, I must add, doubtless did an amount of mischief among the natives that the writer could perhaps hardly realize[1].

[1] I say mischief: for, although the paper (since separately published under the title 'Ideas about India') contains many true and forcible remarks (or, it may be, random shots that occasionally hit the mark), and this may be very salutary reading for some Anglo-Indians, or even for Englishmen at home, if other more thorough books be read in connexion, yet to native readers the whole tone will be most misleading.

As to the passage in Mr W. Scawen Blunt's first paper (*Fortnightly Review*, Vol. xxxvi., p. 175), alluded to in the text, on the luxury of Anglo-Indians, which has given more offence perhaps than any other, if it be appropriate that one cold-weather tourist should rebuke another, I would remind Mr Blunt that it is, to say the least, not always cool in India, and that things that may rank as luxuries here become necessaries of healthy life there. Many of Mr Blunt's most extraordinary statements seem to me simple cases of hasty generalization, which even my own limited observation serves entirely to correct. So far from having found that "no Collector's wife will wear an article of Indian manufacture, to save her soul from perdition" ('Ideas,' p. 29), I got from several kind hostesses many valuable details about Indian clothes and ornaments, which I found that they not only wore themselves but also sent home to their friends in Europe. So far from Englishwomen looking on "the land of their exile as a house of bondage," I have generally found ladies at home preserving the kindest recollections of their Indian life, not excluding the relations with their native servants and dependents. For these, be it observed, are the only natives with whom, as a rule, our countrywomen *can* have much to do, not so much owing to prejudices on their side (though these often doubtless exist), but rather to the barbarous and un-Aryan practice forced upon the Hindus (properly so called) by the ancestors of Mr Blunt's Muhammadan friends. In fact, in those parts of India where Muhammadan rule chiefly prevailed, very few of even the best natives have been at all educated up to the *ideal* of the society of ladies, and for *this* reason, which seems to have escaped Mr Blunt's notice, free social intercourse is out of the question. As a contrast alike to the real average native of a region such as Upper Bengal, and to Mr Blunt's supposed typical Anglo-Indian lady (*ibid.* p. 47), it is a pleasure to me to be able to cite the testimony of an English

But I hope that European residents in India will understand that scholars at least, who start with no preconceived social or political 'ideas' to be proved, can accept the ungrudgingly rendered assistance of their fellow-subjects of every race, without turning it to a root of bitterness and unmerited reproach.

The great kindness shown to me by native scholars has, I trust, been made evident by what I have said in this Report. It was indeed most encouraging to find what a bond of union is formed by enthusiasm for a common study between races sometimes supposed to be almost by nature unblending or even antagonistic. I had not, indeed, expected to find any hostility to my work on the part of the pandits, but in the place of the shy reserve, which even some European scholars accustomed to work like mine had led me to expect, I was often quite surprised at the cordiality and frankness with which both Hindus and Jains came forward to help me. Nor did my native friends and helpers proffer their assistance simply while I was present to ask it, κατ' ὀφθαλμοδουλίαν ὡς ἀνθρωπάρεσκοι; on the contrary, I have received since my return MSS., books and copies of inscriptions from several places that I visited, and scarcely a mail has arrived without bringing me letters from my Indian friends.

To each and all of them, who may chance to read these pages, I can only say, in recording my thanks, that I trust we may meet again before very long, whether some of them may be induced to visit Europe during 1886 from the double attraction of specially Indian celebrations in London and Vienna, or whether I may be permitted to utilise the knowledge and experience I have been gaining by again visiting India.

With such a hope let me conclude. As I have stated in my

lady, the wife of a well-known scholar, who has travelled in many parts of *Western* India amongst the manly Rājputs and the Mahrattas, that she has never met with anything but courtesy from native gentlemen, and that in entertaining, as she often does, the younger members especially of the various higher castes and nationalities (for, *pace* some popular writers and talkers, there is no such thing as '*the* Indian people'), she considers their manners even superior to those cf the corresponding age and class in Europe.

preliminary Report[1], the results described in the foregoing pages need only be regarded, so far as the University is concerned, as a beginning: and for myself I feel that the time and energy which circumstances may leave at my disposal for scholarly work cannot be better employed than in working out at home the material for research thus obtained, in the hope of some day supplementing it by fresh work in the same distant yet pleasant fields.

[1] See the *Cambridge University Reporter* for May 26, 1885, p. 736. Whether used much by myself or by other Sanskritists at Cambridge, I will hope that students in other places will avail themselves of my collection. For (if I may be allowed to repeat an observation made in the preface to my Catalogue of our Buddhist MSS.) the tendency of recent so-called reform has been practically to discourage the prolonged residence in the University of those of its members whose special literary pursuits cannot at once be utilised for the conduct of the ordinary round of its studies; and I fear that it will be some time before Prākrit is studied at our universities in the same way as the Greek and Italian dialects, and perhaps still longer before we may hope for what is already found in some foreign universities, the systematic *comparative* study of religion and philosophy.

PART II.

LISTS OF MSS., WITH NOTES.

I NOW proceed to give an account of what formed the chief object of my journey, the search for MSS.

I therefore give (§ 1) lists of the MSS. collected by myself and of those collected by Pandit Bhagvān Dās and bought together from him, as mentioned above (p. 34).

Of my own MSS., about 212 in number, I have made a classified list. For the Pandit's collection of nearly 300 MSS., I have contented myself with transliterating the very rough list drawn up by or for him. I have corrected a few obvious slips, but I have not had time to verify all names or add dates of writing etc. from the MSS. themselves.

All these, with the exception of a few marked with an asterisk, are now placed at the disposal of the University on terms explained in a Report addressed to the Library Syndicate.

Notes are given (§ 2) on some of the chief MSS. in my own collection. I could have wished, as I have already intimated in the preface, that these could have been fuller and more comprehensive. But I trust that the MSS. may be properly catalogued, along with the valuable collection of Jain MSS. acquired by the University some years ago.

I also give (§ 3) notes on MSS. in India, copies of which might advantageously be negotiated for.

§ 1. CLASSIFIED LIST OF MSS. PERSONALLY COLLECTED.

Contents.

		Number of MSS.
I.	**Veda :**	
	(a) Saṃhitā	2
	(β) Brāhmaṇa	4
	(γ) Sūtra, prayoga, etc.	9
	(δ) Upanishad	6
II.	**Purāṇa**	7
III.	**Itihāsa (epic)**	3
IV.	**Kāvya (belles lettres):**	
	(a) Kāvya (κατ' ἐξοχήν), *i.e.* "artificial" poetry	4
	(β) Nāṭaka (drama)	5
	(γ) Campū	2
	(δ) Kathā (tales)	4
V.	**Vyākaraṇa (grammar)**	6
VI.	**Chandaḥ (metrics) and Alaṅkāra (*ars poetica*)**	5
VII.	**Jyotisha (astronomy and astrology)**	3
VIII.	**Dharmaçāstra (law *etc.*)**	6
IX.	**Art : including**	
	(a) Vaidya (medicine)	1
	(β) Çilpa (constructive art)	2
	(γ) Kāma (*ars amoris*)	3
X.	**Darçana (philosophy) :**	
	(a) General	2
	(β) Sāṅkhya and Yoga	3
	(γ) Nyāya and Vaiçeshika	16
	(δ) Vedānta	30
XI.	**Buddhist works**	12
XII.	**Jain works :**	
	(a) Canonical (§ i. and § ii.)	14
	(β) Extra-canonical	about 60
XII.	**Tantric and miscellaneous works**	4

Total of separate MSS. personally collected, about $\overline{212}$

ABBREVIATIONS.

B.   MSS. acquired in Benares and the North-West Provinces.

N.   „   Nepal.

R.   „   Rājputāna.

* An asterisk, as above stated, indicates that the MS. is reserved and not sent to the University Library.

Note. Except where otherwise stated, all MSS. from Nepal are on palm-leaf, and the rest on paper.

MSS. are arranged under their titles.

The dates of writing are put in the equivalent years of the Christian era.

I. Veda.

(α) *Saṃhitā.*

Anuvākas, collection of. B.

Bhāshya by Uäta on the Ṛikprātiçākhya.

(β) *Brāhmaṇa.*

Çatapatha-brāhmaṇa.—Madhyama-kāṇḍa. 1528. *Imperfect.* B.

Çatapatha-brāhmaṇa.—Hasti-k°. 1582. B.

Taittirīya brāhmaṇa (?), fragm. B.

Vārttika-sāra. B.

(γ) *Sūtra.*

Āpastambīya-sūtra. A *prayoga-vritti* connected with Dhūrtasvāmī's comm. on the A°.; *Praçnas* 1, 2, and part of 3. B.

Pāraskāra-grihya-sūtras. I.—II. 8, xvth cent. palm-leaf, the remainder xviith cent. paper. Wanting 6 lines at end. N.

Paribhāshā. B.

Pavamānahoma-prayoga. 1786. B.

Piṇḍapitṛiyajña-vyatishaṅga by Raghunātha Vājapeyi. 1635. B.

Prāyaçcitta-dīpikā. 1787. B.

Sautrāmaṇi-prayoga. 1786. B.

(δ) *Upanishads.*

Aitareya-upanishad, Çaṅkara's comm. on, 1593. B.

Anubhūtiprakāça (metrical version of the Upanishads) by Vidyāraṇya-svāmī (Sāyaṇa). B.

Bṛihadāraṇyaka-up⁰.   A gloss on Çaṅkara's comm.   B.
Chāndogya-up⁰.   1517.   B.
    ,,   (another copy).   1772.   B.
Māṇḍūkya-up⁰. : Ānandagiri's gloss on Çaṅkara.   B.

II. PURĀṆA.

Agnipurāṇa.   N.
Bhāgavata [one skandha] Bengali hand.   N.
Çivagīta.   B.
Çivapurāṇa followed by Çivadharmottara, xiith cent.   N.
Skanda-p⁰.—Kedāra-khaṇḍa.   1649.   Beng. hand.   N. Paper.
Vishṇupurāṇa.   Beng. hand of xv—xvith cent.   N.
Vṛishasārasaṅgraha.   B (?).

III. ITIHĀSA (Epic).

Mahābhārata : Sabhāparvan.   1693.   N.
    ,,   Udyoga-p⁰ : Sanatsujātīya with Çaṅkara's comm.
          B (?).
Rāmāyana.—Āraṇya-kāṇḍa.   1652.   N.

IV. KĀVYA (Belles lettres).

(α)   *Kāvya.*
    Bhaṭṭi : Sargas I—XIII., with comm. (not Jayamaṅgala's or
        Bharatamallika's) ; Sargas IV—V. Mostly xvth cent.   N.
    Meghadūta, with Sarasvatītīrtha's comm. called Vidvad-
        bālarañjinī.
    Meghadūta with anonymous commentary.   Kashmiri-
        Nāgari writing.
    Sāraṅgasāratattva, circa 1690.   B.
(β)   *Nāṭaka.*
    Anargharāghava (?).   Fragm. of 3 leaves.   Beng. hand,
        xv—xvith cent.   N.
    Çṛiṅgāravāṭikā by Viçvanātha.   B.
    Ekādaçīvrata-nāṭaka, *circa* A.D. 1480.   N.
    Mahāvīracarita.   *Imperf.* xvi—xviith cent. (?).   B.
    Mudrārākshasa.   1376.   N.
(γ)   *Campū.*
    Damayantīkathā (or Nalacampū) by Trivikramabhaṭṭa
        1628.   R.

Damayantīkathāvṛitti (comm.), begun by Candrapāla and finished by Guṇavinayagaṇi. 1853. R.

(δ) *Kathā.*

Hitopadeça [N.S. 493 A.D.] 1373. N.

*Mādhavānalopākhyāna. 1751. N. Paper.

Simhāsanadvātrimçikā; Jainhand (Jain recension?) 1606. R.

*Tantrākhyāna. 1485. N.

V. VYĀKARAṆA (Grammar).

Bhāshyapradīpoddyota. Supercommentary by Nāgojibhaṭṭa on the Mahābhāshya. B.

Cāndravyākaraṇa. See Buddhist works, below, XI.

Dhātupārāyaṇa by Pūrṇacandra. N.

*Kāraka-kaumudī. R.

Prabodhacandrikā by Vaijala. 1857. B.

Samāsavāda by Jayarāma. B.

*Sūtras with comm. not identified. N.

VI. CHANDAḤ AND ALAṄKĀRA (Metrica and ars poetica).

Alaṅkāratilaka or Kavyānuçāsanavṛitti by Vāgbhaṭa.

Devīstotra of Yaçaskara (Çārada character). B.

Prākṛita-piṅgala. (Part of the Piṅgala-çāstra). R.

Rasamañjarī by Bhānumiçra with Gopālabhaṭṭa's comm., Rasika-rañjanī. 1837. B.

Vāgbhaṭālaṅkāra with (new) comm. 1467. R.

VII. JYOTISHA (Astronomy and astrology).

Bālavivekinī with comm. by Nāhnika. 1823. B.

*Tājikasāra by Haribhadra Sūri. 1404. R.

Trivikrama-çata. R.

VIII. DHARMAÇĀSTRA (Law).

Brāhmaṇasarvasva by Halāyudha. B.

Çuddhiviveka by Rudradhara. 1789. R.

Çukranīti. Ch. I. 1851. R.

Kālamādhavīya (fragment). B.

*Nārada-smṛiti with Newari version, and fragments of Newari works. N.

Rājadharmakaustubha, part of Anantadeva's Smṛitikaustubha. B.

IX. Art.

(a) *Vaidya* (medicine).
    Bhīmavinoda (?). *Imperfect.* N.
(β) *Çilpa* (constructive art).
    *Prasādamaṇḍana by Maṇḍana.
    *Viçvakarmaprakāça. B.
(γ) *Kāma* (ars amoris).
    Anaṅgaraṅga by Kalyāṇamalla. 1614. R.
    Ratimañjarī by Jayadeva. R.
    *Vātsyāyana with comm. N.

X. Darçana (Philosophy).

(a) General.
    Sarvadarçana-saṅgraha. B.
    Khaṇḍanoddhāra, supercommentary by Pragalbha Miçra on
        Harsha's Khaṇḍana-khaṇḍa-khādya.
(β) [*Sāṅkhya* and] *Yoga.*
    Haṭhasaṅketacandrikā by Sundara. *Imperf.* 1831. B.
    Yogasūtra with Bhoja's comm. *Imperf.* B.
    Yogavāsishṭasāra with Mahīdhara's comm. B?
(γ) *Nyāya* and *Vaiçeshika.*
    Anyathākhyāti-vicāra (or °-vāda) [by Timmaṇṇa]. B.
    Bādhabuddhivāda by Harirāma Tarkavāgīça. B.
    Dīdhiti-māthurī (cp. Māthurī below). Pt. of § ii. only.
        Comm. on Tattva-cintāmaṇi. *Imperf.* B.
    ' Gaurīkāntī ' Gaurīkānta's comm. on Keçava's Tarkabhāshā.
        B. *Imperf.*
    *' Gaurīkāntī ' (another copy)? complete. B.
    (Vaiçeshika) Guṇakiraṇāvalī-prakāça by Vardhamāna.
        Wants ff. 1—7. B.
    Kiraṇāvalī (?) (Fragment). B.
    Māthurī. Comm. by Mathuranātha on Tattvacintāmaṇi.
        (Part of Khaṇḍa 1 only). Beng. hand XVII—XVIII cent. B.
        Imperf.
    Nirukti. Comm. on Tarkasaṅgraha. Telugu character.
        ? perfect. B.
    Nyāyasiddhāntamañjarī 1760.
    Ratnakoshavāda (?). Defective at end. B.

Saptapadārthī, 1625. R.

Sārasaṅgraha. Comm. on Tārkikarakshā by Varadarāja.
  Ch. I. B.

Tarkaprakāçikā. Comm. by Çitikaṇṭha on Bhaṭṭacārya-
  cūḍāmaṇi's Nyāyasiddhāntamañjarī. 1760. R.

Tātparyavādavicāra. B.

Yogyatāvicāra. B.

(δ) *Vedānta* [and *Mīmāṃsā*].

Advaitasiddhi by Madhusūdana Sūri. B.

Advaitasiddhi, commentary by Brahmānanda. B.

Aparokshānubhūti. Comm. on Çaṅkara's work. B.

*Aparokshānubhūti (another copy). B.

Ātmapurāṇa by Çaṅkarānanda; wanting Ch. 9. 1726. B.

Çrutisāra by Toṭaka with comm. by Saccidānanda Yogi.

Çukāshṭaka with comm. by Gaṅgādharendra Sarasvatī. B.

Gītātātparyabodhinī by Ānandasarasvatī. B.

Jñānasvaprakāça. B.

Kaivalyakalpadruma by Gangādhara Sarasvatī. B.

*Nyāya-makaranda and its ṭīkā (or vivṛiti) by Citsukha
  Muni. Text by Ānandabodha. Kashmiri-Nāgarī character. 1841. B.

Praçnāvalī by Jadubharata. B.

Pañcadaçī III. IV. with Rāmakṛishṇa's Comm. B.
  „   (another copy) I—III. V. B.

Sañjñāprakriyā. B.

Siddhāntaleçasaṅgraha. (End of last chapter wanting). B.
  „   (commentary) defective at end. B.

Siddhāntavindu by Madhusūdana, a comm. on the Daçaçlokī
  B. (?)

Svarūpanirṇaya by Sadānanda. B.

Svātmanirūpaṇa by Çaṅkara, with 'Aryā'-vyākhyā by
  Saccidānanda Sarasvatī. B.

Tattvānusandhāna by Mahādevasarasvatī. B.

Tattvapradīpikā ("Citsukhī"). Jain hand of xvi—xviith
  cent. B.

Upadeçasahasrī with comm. B.

Vairāgyataraṅga. B.

Vākyavṛitti-prakāçikā, comm. on Çaṅkara's Vākya-vṛitti. B.
  *   „   (another copy). B.

Vedānta-kalpataru. B.

Vivekacūḍāmaṇi by Çaṅkara. 1815. B.

A collection of short Vedantic treatises [called Mahā-
vākyaprabodha (?)]. B.

XI. BUDDHIST WORKS. (All from Nepal.)

[1]Ashṭasāhasrikā-prajñāpāramitā. c. A.D. 1020.

"   (another copy).

Cāndravyākaraṇa I—II § ii. and part of II § iii., with comm.
    differing from that of Add. 1657. 1

*Cāndravyākaraṇa...§ 5, 6. In an unknown character.

Kāraṇḍavyūha (prose version). Illuminated. 1196.

Lalitavistara. As to date see notes in Report.

"   (another copy). 1684. (The oldest copy known.) } Paper.

*Pañcarakshā. Palm-leaf (modified Kuṭila writing) with
    modern paper supply. Dated in reign of Vigrahapāla of
    Bengal (c. 1080).

Pañcarakshā (another copy). Archaic hand with more
    recent supply.

[2]Saddharmapuṇḍarīka. 1093. With last leaf of another
    work dated 1065.

Vasudhārā-dhāraṇī. xvth cent.

Fragment of prayers, rituals etc., xivth cent.

XII. JAIN WORKS. (All from Rājputāna.)

(a) *Canonical.*

§ i. *Aṅgas and Upāṅgas.*

Anuttaraupapātikā with Sanskrit glosses.

Prajñāpanā (Paññā°). V.S. 1521 (A.D. 1464).

§ ii. *Other canonical works.*

Aürapaccākkhāṇa ; see below under Saṃstara.

Āvaçyaka-laghuvṛitti : pratikramaṇa-section.

Āvaçyaka. 1534.

Daçavaikālikā with avacūri (A.D. 1400).

---

[1] Lent to Dr Rājendralāla Mitra: deposited at Bengal Asiatic Society,
Calcutta.

[2] Lent to Dr Hörnle: deposited at Bengal Asiatic Society.

*Daçavaikālikā (text only). 1469.

Daçaçrutaskandha. § 8. Paryushaṇākalpa (Padyosavaṇa-
    kappo) 1521.

      ,,   (another copy).   A.D. 1760.

Piṇḍaniryukti.

{Saṃstara followed by
Atura- (Aüra-) pratyākhyāna.

Vyavahāra with comm.   A.D. 1708.

Another work called Paccākhāna (pratyākhyāna).

(β) *Extra-canonical treatises etc.*

    Añjanāsundarī-Yavanakumārasambandha.   1657.

    Anyokti.

    Bandhasāmitta : see below, Shaṭsūtra.

    Çataka   ,,   ,,   ,,

*Çāntināthacaritra.

    Çīlopadeçamālā.

    Çrāvakāṇām mukhavastrikā-rajohāraṇavicāra.   1597.

    Çrāvaka-pratikramaṇa.

    Chandonuçāsana.

    Dharmasaṅgraha by Medhāvin.   (*Imperfect.*)

    Dīpotsava.

    Dravyasaṅgraha by Nemicandra.

    Gotamakulaka.

    Guṇavarmacaritra (Pūjādhikāra).

*Harivaṃça-purāṇa.

    Jīvasamāsa with Çīlācārya's comm.

    Jīvavicāra (by Çāntisāra).

    Kālakācārya-kathā.

        ,,   ,,   (another copy with glosses).   A.D. 1840.

*Kalpāntarvācya (by Ratnacandratilaka) 1638 ;
    with vernacular fragments ; one dated 1672.

    Kalyāṇamandira by Siddhasena.   With comm.

    Karmastava.   }
    Karmavipāka. }   See Shaṭsūtra.

    Kathākoça (Vrata-Kathāk°).

*   ,,   ,,   (another collection ; v. supra, p. 24).

    Laghukshetrasamāsa-vṛitti by Haribhadra.   A.D. 1434.

    Luṃpāka-mata-kuṭṭana.

    Meghanāda-madanamañjarī-kathā.   1552.

Navatattvaprakaraṇa. 1695.

Nemi-purāṇa. 1776.

Pradyumna-carita by Somakīrti.

Pramāṇa-nirṇaya.

Praçnottara ratnamālā with comm.

Ṛishimaṇḍala. 1549.

Sādharaṇajina-stavana by Jayānanda, with comm. 1658.

Sāmbodhipañcāçikā. 1736.

Samyaktvakaumudī. 1695.

Saptatikā
Shaḍaçīti } : see below Shaṭsūtra.

Shaḍāvaçyaka with *bālabodha*.

Shaṭsūtra : the six works are :

 1. Karmavipāka (Kammavibāga).
 2. Bandhasāmitta.
 3. Karmastava.
 4. Shaḍaçīti.
 5. Çataka.
 6. Saptatikā.

Shaṭsūtra (another copy) with comm. on No. 5 and 6.

  „ Commentaries on Nos. 1—4.

Sindūraprakaraṇa. 1843.

    „   (another copy with comm.)

Stotras to Çāntinātha and others. 1698.

Upadeçamālā.

Upadeçarasāla by Sādhuraṅga. 1599.

Vāgbhaṭālaṅkāra. See *Alaṅkāra*.

Vicāramañjarī.

*Vicārasāra.

Vicārashaṭtrimçikā. 1854.

Vivekamañjarī by Āsaḍa.

Yati-ārādhana-vidhi.

Yogaçāstra, comm. by Jinameḍana, pupil of Somasundara.

Several Paṭṭāvalīs.

A treatise by Somasundara, ff. 4, 64 verses.

XII. Tantra, Rituals, and Miscellaneous Works.

Kāraṇḍavyūha : see Buddhist works. N.

Trivikramasundarī or Jñānadīpavimarshiṇī. N.
Anonymous Çivaic work. xiiith cent. N.
Bhuvaneçvarīstotra by Pṛithvīdhara with Padmanābha's
    comm. 1733. R.

ROUGH LIST OF MSS. PURCHASED AT BOMBAY.

Jain MSS.

1. Abhayadeva's comm. on the Antakṛiddaçā.
2. Siddhasena's comm. on the Pravacanasāroddhāra.
3. Abhayadeva's comm. on the Bhagavatisūtra.
4. Abhayadeva's comm. on the Vipāka.
5. Nirayāvalī.
6. Sthānāṅga.
7. Jñātādharmakathā.
8. Uvavāī (Abhayadeva's comm.)
9. Daçavaikālikā.
10. Upadeçamālā.
11. Uttarādhyayana.
12. Ākhyāta-avacūri.
13. Sūtrakṛita.
14. Simhāsanadvātrimçikā (? Jain recension).
15. Kumārasambhava.
16. Padyosavaṇakappa (Paryushaṇā).
17. Rājapraçnīyam.
18. Uttarādhyayana-avacūri.
19. Liṅgānuçāsana-avacūri.
20. Jīvābhigama.
21. Sūryaprajñapti.
22. Padyosavaṇa with *tippaṇi*.
23. Praçnavyakaraṇa with Abhayadeva's comm.
24. Piṇḍa...avacūri.

25. Yogaçāstra.
26. Çāntinātha-caritra.
27. Ācārāṅga.
28. Daçavaikālika.
29. Malayagiri's comm. on Rājapraçnīya.
30. Abhayadeva's comm. on Upāsakadaçā.
31. Āvaçyaka-avacūri.
32. Pushpamālā.
33. Antakṛiddaçā with comm.
34. Jñātādharmakathā.
35. Sūtrakṛita (niryukti).
36. Kalpasūtra-avacūri.
37. Abhidhānacintāmaṇi of Hemacandra.
38. Laghu-saṅgrahaṇī-ratna.
39. Bhagavatī.
40. Kalpa-kiraṇāvalī.
41. Pārçvanāthacaritra.
42. Jīvābhigama.
43. Pākshika.
44. Vallabhadeva's comm. on Kumāra-sambhava.
45. Abhayadeva's comm. on Jñātādharma-kathā.
46. Arādhana-sūtra.
47. Pratikramaṇa-sūtra.
48. Yogaçāstra.
49. Jambudvīpaprajñapti.
50. Abhidhānacintāmaṇi comm.
51. Antakṛiddaçā.

52. Kshetrasamāsa.
53. Rishimaṇḍala.
54. Dhātupāṭha with comm.
55. Oghaniryukti.
56. Kalyāṇamandira with comm.
57. Anuttaraupapātika.
58. Kalpāntarvācyāni (A.D. 1457).
59. Prajñāpanā.
60. Praudhamanorama.
61. Çabdānuçāsana (imperf.)
62. Varāhī saṃhitā (part only).
63. Çabdānuçāsana, pt. 2. (Saṃv. 1482).
64. Çabdānuçāsana, pt. 8.
65. Liṅgānuçāsana (Hemacandra)
66. Çabdānuçāsana, pt. 4.
67.   ,,   pt. 2 (2 leaves wanting).
68. Çabdāvacūrṇi pt. 1.
69.   ,,   pt. 2.
70. Çabdānuçāsana pt....?
71.   ,,   pt. 1.
72.   ,,   pt. 5.
73.   ,,   pt....?
74.   ,,   pt....?
75. Ākhyātāvacūrṇi.
76. Prajñāpanā with comm.
77. Dharmabuddhi-kathā (?).
78. Āturapratyākhyāna.
79. Taṇḍula-vaiyālika.
80. Sūktamuktāvalī-ṭīkā.
81. Samavāyāṅga.
82. Candraprajñapti.
83. Vītarāgastotra.
84. Çabdānuçāsana-vṛitti, pts. 1 and 2.

85. Kalpāntarvācyāni (cf. 58).
86. Āvaçyaka.
87. Sarvajanopadeça.
88. Laghusaṅgrahaṇī with comm.
89. Bhavabhāvanā (Hemacandra).
90. Paramātmaprakāça.
91. Shaḍḍarçanasaṅgraha.
92. Kriyākalāpa.
93. Jambudvīpasaṅgrahaṇī with comm.
*94. Rohiṇī-Açokanripa-kathā.
95. Çrāddha- pratikramaṇa-sūtra-vṛitti.
96. Munipaticarita.
97. Dhātupāṭha.
98. Navatattva.
99. [Tales.]
100. Çabdānuçāsana, comm. (Part of Adhy. V.).
101. Yogaçāstra.
102. Ācārāṅga-sūtra-vṛitti (Çīlāṅgāchārya).
103. Pratyākhyāna-bhāshya.
104. Samyaktvakaumudī.
105. Shashṭi-çataka.
106. Kshetrasamāsa-avacūri.
107. Āvaçyaka-avacūri.
108. Pratyākhyāna-bhāshya with avacūri.
*109. Kūrmaputra-kathā.
110. Adhyātmasāra.
111. Vidagdhamukhamaṇḍana-ṭīkā.
112. Vicārashaṭṭrimçikā.
113. Sthirāvalī.
114. Guṇasthānavivaraṇa.
*115. Gurvāvali with comm.
116. Dravyasaṅgraha.

117. Gautama-pricchā.
118. Saṅgrahaṇī with comm.
119. Çabdānuçāsana (Adhy. V.).
120. Shaḍāvaçyaka.
121. Jambūcaritra (with praçasti, slightly imperfect).
122. Divālīkalpa (?).
123. Çabdānuçāsana (Adhy. III).
124. Saptatisthāna.
*125. Campakaçreshṭhi-kathā.
*126. Maunaikādaçī-māhātmya.
127. Vipāka sūtra.
128. Kālakācārya-kathā.
129. Āvaçyaka-niryukti-ṭīkā.
130. Navatattva with comm.
131. Nandī-vritti.
132. Anekārthasaṅgraha with comm. ; *imperfect.*
*133. Sambodha-sattarikā.
134. Bhaktāmara with comm.
135. Anushṭhānasubodha (*imperf.*).
136. Samācārīçataka.
137. Trishashṭiçatakapurusha-caritra (part of).
138. Khaṇḍapraçasti.
139. Pratyākhyāna-niryukti.
140. Jñānārṇavayogapradīpa.

Brahmanical and general MSS.

141. Narapati-jayacaryā.
142. A collection of Upanishads.
143. Vritabadha-paddhāti.
144. Vedānta-paribhāshā.
145. Tājika-sāra.
146. Anekārthadhvani-mañjarī.
147. Prabodhacandrodaya.
148. Holāshṭaka.

149. Siddhāntamuktāvalī.
150. Strījātaka.
151. Vedāntasāra.
152. Bhuvanadīpaka.
153. Nīlakaṇṭha-tājika.
154. Smritisārasamuccaya (*imperf.*)
155. Kaivalyopanishad.
156. Pratishṭhā° kalanirṇaya.
157. Dhātupāṭha.
158. Makarandāharaṇa.
159. Praçna-vaishṇava.
160. Bhojaprabandha.
161. Brihaj-jātaka.
162. Ramalacintāmaṇī.
163. Tājikapaddhati with comm.
164. Sarvasaṅgraha.
165. Uäta-bhāshya (*imperf.*)
166. Raghuvaṃça-comm.
167. Sārasvata, Mādhava-ṭikā.
168. Çāradātilaka (*imperf.*)
169. Ghaṭapartha-kāvya.
170. Dhātupāṭha.
171. Gaṅgā-pīyūshalaharī.
172. Pratishṭhāmayūkha.
173. Vākyasudhā.
174. Laghujātaka.
175. Ajapāgāyatrī.
176. Jātakapaddhati.
177. Ramalapraçna.
178. Upākarmapaddhati.
179. Nighaṇṭu.
180. Rasamañjarī.
181. Makaranda-ṭippaṇa.
182. Siddhānta-muktāvalī.
183. Çriṅgāratilaka with comm.
184. Vasishṭha-çānti (Saṃv. 1510).
185. Pratyaṅgira-kavaca.

186. Rasamañjarī.
187. Caraṇavyūha.
188. Asaucanirṇaya.
189. Pañcaviveka.
190. Vaidyamanorama.
191. Triçatī by Çārṅgadhara.
192. Ashtavakra with comm.
193. Amaranāmamālā.
194. Bhārata-tilaka.
195. Parāçara-smriti.
196. Vetālapañcaviṃçati.
197. Vishṇusahasra-nāma-bhā-shya.
198. Ācārādarça.
199. Indraprasthamāhātmya.
200. Brahmasūtra.
201. Prāyaçcitta-mayūkha.
202. Çrāddha-mayūkha.
203. Vishṇu-purāṇa.
204. Naishadha - commentary (Çāradā character).
205. Ghatakarpara with comm.
206. Makaranda-vivaraṇa.
207. Nyāya-siddhāntamañjari.
208. Pāṇini's Ashtādhyāyī (from Kashmir).
209. Kuvalayānanda, comm.
209 a. Garuḍopanishad-dīpikā (Kashmir).
209 b. Amarakosha (Çāradā cha-racter).
210. Hemādri, Pariçesha-khan-ḍa (imperf.).
211. Veda raçārtha (?) (Çāradā).
212. Jñānārṇava (*imperf.*).
213. Çabdabodha.
214. Vrihad-naradīya-purāṇa (unfinished).
215. Anekārtha-mañjarī.

216. Māgha-durghaṭa.
217. Yājñavalkya-comm. (*imp.*).
218. Durghaṭa-kāvya with comm.
219. Lagnabrāhmaṇa (60 çlo-kas).
220. Arthavivecana.
221. Mahimna-stotra with comm.
222. Rudrabhāshya (Çāradā).
223. Laghukaumudī (Çāradā, *imperf.*).
224. Āçvalāyana-grihyasūtra.
225. Kaularahasya.
226. Lalita-paramarahasya (Çāradā).
227. Kāvya-subhāshita.
228. Sambandha-viveka.
229. Rājamārtaṇḍa (*imperf.*).
230. Nilotsarga-vidhi (*imperf.*).
231. Mātrikā-nighaṇṭu.
232. Dharmopastava - khaṇḍana by Vedāntavāgīça Ācā-rya.
233. Grahaçānti.
234. Mīmāṃsā-rahasya (one adhyāya only).
235. Siddhānta-candrikā.
236. Ashtavakra-comm.
237. Amarakosha-comm.
238. Çārṅgadhara (medical).
239. Pañcadaçī (with comm.)
240. Suçruta.
241. Chāndogya-upanishadviva-raṇa (*imperf.*).
242. Anuvāka.
243. Yogārṇava.
244. Nyāya-çāstra.
245. Nirṇayasindhu.

246. Jātakābharaṇa.
247. Vājasaneyī.
248. Vṛihaj-jātaka.
249. Çaṭacaṇḍī-paddhati.
250. Mṛityuñjaya-japavidhi (*imperf.*).
251. Cintāmaṇi comm.
252. Rasarāja.
253. Vīramitrodaya, comm.
254. Pasakakevalī (?).
255. Muhūrtacintāmaṇi, comm.
256. Cāturmāsyavṛita.
257. Nītimayūkha.
258. Çrāddhaviveka.
259. Mahimna with comm.
260. Nāciketa-upākhyāna.
261. Muhūrtamārtaṇḍa.
262. Raghuvaṃça.
263. Laghusiddhāntakaumudī.
264. Vishṇubhaktikalpalatā.
265. Nyāyamañjarī.
266. Kumārārtha-vivecana by Ekanātha.
267. Rāmakṛishṇavilāpa-kāvya.
268. Mahārudra-paddhati.
269. Nāgara-khaṇḍa (*imperf.*).
270. Punarārādhana-nimittāni.
271. Kaiyyata's comm. on the Mahābhāshya.

272. Māgha-kāvya, comm.
273. Sāmavedasaṃhitā (*imp.*).
274. Cāṇakya (*imp.*).
275. Jātaka-paddhati with comm.
276. Çīghrabodha.
277. Vṛittaratnākara, comm.
278. Muktāvalī-prakāça.
279. Samara-sāra.
280. Kāvya-prakāça (*imperf.*).
281. Ṭabba-cintāmaṇi (?).
282. Çatapatha-brāhmaṇa (fragment of 1000 çlokas).
283. Rasāyana-tantra.
284. Āçvalāyana-brāhmaṇa (?).
285. Jātakakarma-paddhati.
286. Çatapatha-brāhmaṇa (850 çlokas).
287. Yogaçataka.
288. Tulasī-vivāha.
289. Yogavāsishṭha (fr. of 400 çlokas).
290. Vāradarājīya-vyākhyāna (*imperf.*).
291. Jyotishaçlokāḥ (500 çl.).
292. Gītagovinda.
293. Muhūrtamārtaṇḍa.
294. Çabdakaustubha.

§ 2. NOTES ON PARTICULAR MSS. ACQUIRED.

(1) FROM NEPAL.

I regret that I have little of fresh interest in Buddhist literature. There will be found however several fresh MSS. of works already known, as well as several non-Buddhistic works of some importance.

A partial exception may be noted in the case of the *Cāndra-vyākaraṇa* or grammar of the Cāndra school of grammarians, attributed to Candragomin, a Buddhist author. Of the text and its commentaries our library already possesses several portions, which are duly noted in the Catalogue.

I have now secured several new fragments of this work.

The first of these (List, XI, 4) has the great interest of being written in a character unknown to me and, I may say, unknown in India also, for I showed the MS. or a specimen of the character to all the chief authorities in such matters, both European and native, in Northern India.

In the Calcutta Museum however I observed a figure of Buddha on a pedestal inscribed with characters somewhat more difficult to decipher than those of my MS. (indeed I learned from the Curator that the inscription never had been read), but still bearing the same distinguishing feature : namely, a triangular ornament at the top of each vertical stroke in the letters. The form of letter with thick tops tapering down into a quasi-triangular form is well known, but here we get the apex of the triangle uppermost. Besides this there are many very curious archaisms in the letters themselves.

I have obtained a photograph of the figure above-mentioned, and with the help of this and of my squeezes and rubbings I hope to be able to publish a complete study of this character before long.

Parāsara-grihya-sūtra. Vedic texts seem to be rare in Nepal. There seems to be little of consequence in this literature even in the great Durbar library. The owner of the present MS. evidently had no idea of what it was, as he described the book in a list that he sent to me simply as '*chotā-wālā*' "little one." Parāsara-grihya-sūtra.

Mahābhārata.—Sabhāparvan. This MS. is remarkable as being by far the latest Nepalese palm-leaf I have met with. The colophon records that it was written "for the hearing [*i.e.* so that the book might be read to] King Yoganarendra Malla, by the Bengali Brahman Harihara in Nepal saṃvat 813 (A.D. 1693)." Mahābhārata.

Hitopadeça and *Mudrārākshasa.* These books were written by the same scribe at an interval of three years, N.S. 493—6 (A.D. 1373—6). It is I think of some importance for the history of the Hitopadeça, which has usually been regarded as a somewhat late redaction of the great collection of the Pañca-tantra, to find that in the middle of the xivth century it had already gained enough celebrity to be copied in the valley of Nepal. Hitopadeça and Mudrārākshasa.

I also acquired a large MS. which was stated by its owner to be the Bhīmavinoda. Unfortunately, the book is imperfect at both ends, and I can find no clue to its name in any chapter-title; nor could I get any assistance in recognising the work from various pandits to whom I showed it in other parts of India. Part of an index remains. This begins with the treatment of special diseases (*jvarātīsāra*, 'fever and dysentery' fol. 66 of original MS.) and ends with various general modes of treatment (*dhūmapāna — kavaḍa — nasyādi* "smoke-inhaling, rinsing, sternutatories" ff. 528—531). A large fragment of a medical work said to be theBhīmavinoda.

I obtained another copy of the *Tantrākhyāna*, a work already in the Wright collection. It is a collection of tales, of which many, but not all, occur in the Pañca-tantra and Hitopadeça. The work deserves investigation in connexion with the studies in Indian folk-lore now in progress in several quarters. It consists of 43 short stories, chiefly in verse. The Tantrākhyāna.

first is of the tortoise and the two geese; the second, the prince and the ape.

In the same covers, and written by the same scribe 'Jasa'-varmā, is a quasi-dramatic piece on the *Ekādaçī-vrata* or the vow of the eleventh day, composed (fol. 4, *a* 4) for king Jaya-ratna Malla.

Tripura-sundarī of Vidyā-nanda-nātha. The *Tripurasundarā-paddhati* or *Jñānadīpavimarshinī* is an unknown Sivaic ritual-book by an unknown author, Vidyā-nandanātha or °nāthadeva, described as *Mahāpadmavana-shanda-vihārī*. A full alphabet is given on f. 74 *b*.

Anonymous work. Another work is remarkable as being by far the smallest palmleaf MS. yet found in Nepal, as it measures only $5 \times 1\frac{1}{2}$ inches. It has no title and I have not succeeded in identifying it. It is divided into 28 *adhyāyas*, and commences with a dialogue between Çiva and Parvatī.

Nārada. I now give some extracts from a very full description kindly supplied to me by Professor Jolly of Würzburg of a fragment obtained by me in Nepal, which has turned out to be a new recension of the Nārada-smriti. My discovery of this MS. has been most opportune, as he is at present printing a critical edition of the text as a fitting sequel to his valuable translation of this *dharma-çāstra*.

The first portion of the MS. "The Nepalese MS. of the Nārada-smriti is very valuable indeed, both on account of its marked divergence from all the other MSS. of that work, that have come to light hitherto, and on account of its age. It is dated, at the end, N. S. 527, whereas none of the other MSS. is more than a hundred years old. The first portion of the Nepalese Nārada has apparently been lost and supplanted by fragments of two different works in the Nepalese language, the first of which extends from fol. 1 to fol. 24*a*, and is written in a very clear hand. It is described at the end as a Nepalese commentary on a Nyāyaçāstra (*iti nīnāmakṛitanyāyaçāstranepalabhāshāṭipini samāptaḥ*), and dated 527, like the fragment of Nārada. Fol. 24*b* and fol. 27 (25 and 26 are missing), seem to contain fragments of another

Nepalese composition. They are very badly written. The fragment of the Nārada-smṛiti, accompanied by a commentary in Nevari, is written in yet another hand, and begins at fol. 28 *a* with the words: *vṛittir eshā dāreshu guruputre tathaiva ca* ‖, which correspond to the latter portion of paragr. 8, V. Head of Dispute, in the Indian MSS., and in my English translation of the Institutes of Nārada. The following leaves, up to fol. 93, agree in the main with the Indian recension, as contained in my translation and in the edition which I am printing, from seven Indian MSS., in the *Bibliotheca Indica.*"

[Prof. Jolly here subjoins a most valuable list of various readings, which I omit as being beyond the scope of the present work, and also because I trust his edition will shortly appear.]

"It will be seen from the list of various readings that the Nepalese MS. is a valuable check on the Indian MSS. of Nārada. In many cases, the superior correctness of its readings admits of direct proof through the numerous quotations from the Nārada-smṛiti, which are scattered through the Mitāksharā, Vīramitrodaya, and other Commentaries and Digests of Law. It is true that in a number of other cases the quotations speak in favour of the readings preserved in the Indian recension of Nārada. The Nepalese MS. is also by no means free from serious blunders.

"The last Vivādapada, called Prakīrṇaka, does not however constitute the final chapter of the Nepalese, as it does of the Indian, Nārada. It is followed, first, at fol. 93 *b*, by a long chapter on Theft or Caurapratishedha, as it is called in the colophon (*nāradaproktāyām caurapratishedham nāma prakaraṇam samāptam*). The opening çlokas of this chapter agree very closely with Manu IX. 256—260. The remainder has its counterpart both in Manu IX. 252—293, and in the eighth chapter of the Code of Manu, where the subject of Theft is treated at considerable length (VIII. 301—343). It may seem strange that an additional chapter on Theft should thus be introduced at the close of the whole work, after all the eighteen Vivādapadas have been discussed in their order. Precisely the same want of consistency is, however, observable in Manu's treatment of forensic law, a chapter on Theft and kindred matters being tacked on, at the close of the section on forensic law, in the Code of Manu as well as in the present text. This fact goes far to prove the genuineness of the chapter on Theft in the Nepalese MS. It is also important, because it gives fresh support to the truth of the traditional statements, which connect the composition of the Nārada-smṛiti with the Code of Manu. Indian tradition is wrong, it is true, in making the Nārada-smṛiti an early recension of the Code of Manu. The chapter on Theft, as well as the entire previous portion of the book, is full of detailed rules and provisions, which are decidedly less archaic than the corresponding rules of Manu. It consists of no less than 61 çlokas and one trishṭubh. Moreover, it contains a reference to a coin called *dīnāra*, which corresponds to the Latin *denarius*[1]. Some texts from this chapter are expressly attributed to Nārada in the Vīramitrodaya.

e final
apter on
leals. "It is more difficult to account for the addition, at fol. 106 *b* of the Nepalese MS., of a final chapter on Ordeals, which subject is usually treated in the law of evidence.

e end. "At fol. 118 *a* the whole work closes as follows: idam alpadhiyāṃ nṛīṇāṃ durvijñeyaṃ yathoditam | nāradīyam yad astīha nyāyaçāstraṃ mahārthavat || tasyeyaṃ likhyate ṭīkā spashṭā nepālabhāshayā | imāṃ vijñāya bhūpādyāç carantu nyāyavartmanā || ° || iti mānave nyāyaçāstre nāradaproktāyāṃ saṃhitāyāṃ nyāyadharmapadāni samāptāni || ꙩ || saṃvat 527 kārttikamāse, etc. The last clause, which contains the date, is written in different hand from the remainder of the work, and very indistinctly. The colophon, in accordance with some of the previous colophons, describes the work of Nārada as a recension of the Code of Manu. This tends to confirm the Indian tradition, above referred to, regarding the connexion of Manu with Nārada. See, too, my *Tagore Law Lectures*, pp. 46 and 57. It is curious that the Code of Manu is called a Nyāyaçāstra in the last colophon. The term *nyāya* in this compound is no

---

[1] Regarding the occurrence of this term in the previous portion of the Nārada-smṛiti, see West and Bühler's *Digest of Hindu Law*, 3rd ed., p. 48 and Jolly, *Tagore Law Lectures* (Calcutta 1885, Thacker and Spink), p. 56.

doubt an equivalent for *dharma*, as is not seldom the case in the law-books, e.g. Nārada XVII. 9. The same use of the term recurs in the two çlokas just quoted, in which the author of the Nepalese Commentary declares that he has written it for the enlightenment of kings and others, as the Nārada-smṛiti is difficult for the ignorant to understand."

(2) General Collection (Benares, Rajputana, etc.).
Kāvya (Poetry, etc.).

Though six commentaries on the Meghadūta are made known to us by Aufrecht (*Bodl. Catal.* p. 125), I have acquired two copies of the text with commentaries hitherto, as far as I know, unnoticed. Two Commentaries on the Meghadūta.

The MSS. give the text in somewhat different forms, as the first has 122 distichs and the second 113, while the Oxford copy above cited has 116. Two of the spurious verses noted by Aufrecht (आनन्दोत्यं and आश्वखिनां, here given as आश्वखिवं,) occur in the first MS. as vv. 71 and 118 respectively. The commentary to this MS., called Vidvadbālānurañjinī, was written at Benares by Sarasvatītīrtha, called in the commentary itself 'Yati' and in the colophon 'Paramahaṃsa Parivrājakācārya.'

In the second MS. the name of the commentator is not given in the colophon. He thus refers to himself and his work in verses 2 and 3 :

कालिदासवचः कुच व्याख्यातारौ वयं क्व च ।

तदिदं मंददीपेन राजवेश्मप्रकाशनं ॥

तथापि क्रियतेऽस्माभिर्मेघदूतस्य पंचका ।

उन्नताश्रयमाहात्म्यस्वरूपख्यातिलालसैः ॥

This MS. is written in the fine bold form of Nāgari for which the scribes of Kashmir are celebrated. An antique Kashmirian form of घ may be noted in leaf 1 line 4, in the third of the lines just quoted. Several other good examples of this writing, besides one instance[1] of the old Kashmirian or Çāradā, may be found in the present collection. In the Jeypore royal library I found one Kashmirian copyist at work.

Māgha-durghata.

À propos of commentaries on the *Kāvyas* I may call attention in passing (though this is included in the collection of MSS. from Bombay [No. 216] which I am not able at present to describe) to a collection of short adversaria on the Māgha-kāvya called *Māgha-durghata*, by one Rājakrūḍa.

Sāraṅga-sāra-tattva.

Sāraṅgasāratattva. This is a collection of 200 verses on polity or general morality. In spite of the strange form of the title it would seem to be compiled from the Çārṅgadhara-paddhati. The last clause runs: माकन्दादिव मञ्जरी घनभरावर्षेवया निर्गता सेयं श्रार्ङ्गधरात्तनोतु जगतां चेतोमुदं पद्धति: । Though obtained at Benares, the MS. was written for the Maharāṇa Jayasimha, who reigned at Oodeypore A.D. 1680—99.

Nala-campū, comm.

In the special form of poetical composition called *campū*, I obtained a MS. of a *tippana* or commentary on the Damayantīkathā or Nala-campū by two Jains, Candapāla and Guṇavinaya Gaṇi, with a *pattāvalī* of these commentators.

Nāṭaka (Drama).

Çriṅgāra-vāṭikā.

Under this head I have a portion of a play, the *Çriṅgāra-vāṭikā,* or 'love-garden,' produced for Vishṇusimha, *Kumāra* of the Mahārāja Rāmasimha, doubtless the sovereign of Jeypore, whom we noticed above (p. 28), as a patron of the drama. Of the 29 remaining leaves (for the leaf numbered 30, placed with the rest, does not belong to this MS.), 10 are occupied with the prologue, from which we learn (f. 5 *a*) that the story tells of Candraketu son of Vijayaketu, king of Avantī, who left his kingdom to the care of his minister Buddhisāgara and travelled to Campāvatī. The first scene discovers him with his companion, the Vidūshaka; his adventures are described in the garden of Kāntimatī daughter of Ratnapāla, king of that city (f. 15 *a*—*b*).

---

[1] This is a copy of the *Devīstotra* of Yaçaskara; see p. 43 above, Sect. VI.

Alaṅkāra (Rhetoric and *ars poetica*).

Under this head we have a copy of the *Vāgbhaṭālaṅkāra* Vāgbhaṭa with an anonymous commentary not previously, I think, noticed. with comm. In it we find Vāgbhaṭa called by a Prakritized form of name, Bāhaḍa or Bāhaḍadeva. The subscription of Chapter IV. runs:

दूति बाहडमंत्रीश्वरविरचितवाग्मटालंकारे चतुर्थः परिच्छेद:

and in the final subscription the author is styled मंत्रि वाग्मट; so that we may perhaps infer that he was the minister of the king Jayasimha (cf. Aufrecht, *Bodleian Catalogue*, 214 *a*), under whom the work was composed. The commentator identifies this king with the son of Karṇadeva cited by Aufrecht.

The MS., which is a good specimen of Jain calligraphy, was written in V.S. 1524 (A.D. 1467) during the pontificate of Lakshmīsāgara of the Tapāgaccha, who attained his *sūripada* in V.S. 1508 (see Klatt in *Ind. Ant.* XI. 256).

I have also obtained a copy of the *Alaṅkāratilaka* (cf. Alaṅkāra tilaka. Bühler, *Cat. MSS. Gujarat*, III. 44). A second title of the book is *Kāvyānuçāsana*. This is likewise the work of a Vāgbhaṭa, who from the introduction is clearly a Jain and in the postscript is described as famed for 'the composition of several new works'

(नव्यानेक महाप्रबन्धरचना). He may thus be fairly identified with the author of the Vāgbhaṭālaṅkāra; but being also described as the son of Nemīkumāra, he must be separated[1] from the medical Vāgbhaṭa, who was the son of Simhagupta and named after his grandfather Vāgbhaṭa[2].

A third work among my few, but on the whole interesting, Rasa-mañ- specimens of Alaṅkāra-literature is Bhānudatta's *Rasamañjarī* jarī with with a commentary called Rasikarañjanī by Gopāla Bhaṭṭa, son of comm. Harivamça Bhaṭṭa. This MS. supports the reading विदेहम्‌ :, noticed by Professor Rāmkrishṇa Bhāṇḍārkar (Report on Sk.

---

[1] In spite of the tradition referred to by Burnell, *Cat. Tanjore*, 57 *b*.

[2] See the verse quoted from the physician's own writings by Anna Moreçvara Kunte in the preface (p. 6) to his edition of the Ashtāṅgahridaya, which may be taken in modification of Prof. Aufrecht's statement that Vāgbhaṭa's parentage is 'subscriptionibus tantum librorum traditum' (*Cat. Bodl.* p. 303, not.).

MSS. 1882—3) as giving the right indication of the author's birth-place.

Darçana (Philosophy).

Various Vedantic works. *Praçnāvalī*, by Jadubharata, pupil of Mādhavānanda; a catechism of Vedantic doctrine.

Svarūpanirṇaya a Vedantic work on the nature of *ātman* by Sadānanda, clearly the same as that mentioned by Hall (*Index*, p. 129) though this copy has about 2000 çlokas as compared with 800 in Hall's. My MS. has four chapters (*pariccheda*), the last being entitled *jīvanmuktibhūmikānirūpaṇa*.

Svātmanirūpaṇa by Çaṅkarācārya. The commentary by Saccidānanda Sarasvatī, which is mentioned without any special name by Hall (p. 104), is given, and styled Āryā-vyākhyā.

Çrutisāra, by Toṭakācārya, said to have been a pupil of Çaṅkara. The only other known copy of this work seems to be a MS. at Tanjore (Burnell, p. 95 *a*). The work consists of 160 çlokas; and our MS. has a commentary by Saccidānanda Yogi, 'Yogīndra-çishya,' of which I have found no trace elsewhere.

The *Saṃjñāprakriyā* is a short compendium of Vedantic terminology which may prove useful to the lexicographer as well as to the student of philosophy. I have not found mention of the work in any catalogue of MSS.

The *Gītātātparyabodhinī* is a Vedantic commentary on the Bhagavadgītā by Ānandasarasvatī, an author of whom nothing appears to be known. The present MS. contains *adhyāyas* I. II. VII. VIII. and part of IX.

Jain works.

Sambodhi-pañcāsikā. This is a tract of 50 verses in Prakrit on *saṃsāra*, the *dharma* and other teachings of Jainism, in the form of instruction given to a pupil by the author, Gotama Svāmī. Each verse is accompanied by a paraphrase in Sanskrit.

It would be interesting to know why we find in the text the month, in the commentary the month and day, but in neither the year, when the book was composed.

Dharmasaṅgraha. This is a work in verse on various religious topics by Medhāvin, who describes himself as Çrī-Jinacandrānte-vāsī. In Ch. I. verse 6 we find a reference to श्रीजिनसेनकः ..कर्त्ता महापुराणस्य. After some verses on cosmogony the chapter concludes with a legend of king Çreṇika, its title being 'Çreṇikānandavarṇana.' At f. 11 are some descriptions of the architecture and decorations of shrines.

The *Pramāṇanirṇaya* is a discussion of the various kinds of *pramāṇa*, or sources of knowledge, after the manner of the ordinary philosophical works. The chief divisions of the work are on *lakshana*, *pratyaksha*, and *anumāna* (fol. 31 a). In the chapter which appears (for the MS. is unfortunately incomplete) to be the last, we find an inquiry into the authority of the *āgamas* which form to the Jain philosopher *çabda* or the ' Word.' The text is written in a fine bold hand and is accompanied by brief marginal glosses containing references to Jain literature, *e.g.* the Vītarāgakathā (f. 31 a), and to Buddhist teaching (ff. 28 b, 31 a).

Lumpāka-mata-kuṭṭana is the subscription of a short work (of 21 leaves). Outside is written in a much later hand 'Lokāyata-kuṭṭana.' The Lumpāka mata was a school founded in Vikr. Saṃvat 1508 (A.D. 1461). See Dr Klatt in *Ind. Antiq.* XI. 256 (September 1882). The treatise is in the main a compilation from the Siddhānta or canon of the Çvetāmbaras and begins : नत्वा श्रुतज्ञानमनंतभेदं । पारंगतं चेतसि सन्निधाय । सिद्धान्त-वाक्यानि करोमि सम्यक् । Its compilers belonged to the Kharatara-gaccha and wrote the work in Saṃvat 1687.

Another work of similar dimensions and date is the *Upadeçarasāla* by Sādhuraṅga pupil of Bhuvanasoma, (also of the Kharatara-gaccha) composed in V. S. 1587 (A.D. 1530). The MS. was written in Saṃvat 1656 (A.D. 1599), during Jinacandra's pontificate. The subject is ethical, and the language Sanskrit with Prakrit citations.

On various subjects connected with religious ordinances and discipline we have a *Vicāra-saṅgraha* or *Paramita-vicārā-mṛita saṅgraha*, being a collection of 25 *vicāras* (examinations ?).

The title of the first is *Jinapravacana-svarūpa-vicāra*. The last relates to the ground-whisks and 'respirators' (मुखवस्त्रिकारजोहरण) to prevent the destruction of insect life, which I saw myself in actual use among Jain monks. The work is in Sanskrit, with numerous citations from the canonical, and other Prakrit, books.

Another work not previously noticed, I think, is the *Vicārasāraprakaraṇa* or *Mārgaṇaçataka*, of 117 Prakrit verses, with a very full Sanskrit commentary, terminating with a paṭṭāvalī of the Kharatara-gaccha.

I also collected, wherever I could, *Paṭṭāvalīs* (lists of Jain pontiffs and teachers). The publication of several such lists by Dr Klatt in the *Indian Antiquary* for 1882 has proved most useful. I hope to publish those that I have collected, and trust that we may in time thus get material for a regular table of Jain chronology, which cannot fail to be of the greatest use for general Indian history.

In the extensive literature of Jain folk-lore a new acquisition is the *Guṇavarmacaritra*, a work in Sanskrit verse by Maṇikya-sundara Sūri of the Añcala-gaccha, the author of the Pṛthvī-candacarita, of which a MS. exists in the Berlin library. For purposes of identification, especially as the work has another title in the margin, *Çatarabhedaka*[thā ?], I may mention that the opening of the tale relates how Guṇavarmā son of Naravarmā, king of Hastināpur, and Līlavatī his queen go to the *svayaṃvara* of Guṇāvalī daughter of the king of Campā (Bhagalpur). The moral of the tale is the duty of proper religious observance (*pūjā*).

Another large collection of tales is the *Vratakathākoça* or *Vratopākhyāna-kathā* composed by Çrutisāgara, *Bhaṭṭā-raka-Çrī-Mallibhūshaṇa-bhaṭṭārakagurūpadeçāt*. It consists of 24 stories in numbered Sanskrit verses, related in order to illustrate the merit of observing fasts and holy-days. Numerous parallels to this are to be found in the Buddhist literature of Nepal, as for example the tale in praise of the Ashṭamī-vrata (*Catal.* pp. 15, 73). The first tale of the present series is called Jyeshtha-jinakathā.

Similar to this collection is a tale in 150 verses of which the colophon runs: *iti çrī-kārttike saubhāgyapañcamīmāhātmya-vishaye Varadatta-Guṇamañjarī-kathānakam.*

The *Jaya-tihuyaṇa* (tribhuvana)-*vṛitti* is a Prakrit hymn in 30 verses with a Sanskrit commentary and an introductory tale told in Sanskrit, of the sickness, nocturnal vision, cure and subsequent votive offering of Abhayadeva Sūri at Sthambana(-ka)-pur in Gujarat.

Varadatta-
Guṇa-
mañjarī-
kathā.

Jaya-ti-
huyaṇa-
vṛitti.

§ 3. NOTES ON MSS. IN PRIVATE POSSESSION, NOT ACQUIRED, OF WHICH COPIES COULD BE MADE FOR THE LIBRARY.

Besides the MSS. in the great libraries of Kathmandu and Jeypore, and those in the Government College Library at Benares, of which some account has been given in Part I., I noted a number of MSS. of which copies could be made for the Library, or actually had been made. Indeed it was my constant endeavour to induce owners of books to show me all the good MSS. they possessed, whether they were willing to part with them in every case or not.

In Nepal I was offered a copy of the *Bhadrakalpāvadāna*. As I had not sufficient data to show whether this was not a copy made by the owner previous to the sale of an original to Dr D. Wright (Add. 1411, Catalogue, p. 88), I declined to purchase it. But I am not sure whether the MS. might not be worth purchasing, even with this risk, owing to its rarity and interest.

At Benares I examined the following MSS., of which the owner would willingly send copies, made at the rate of 2 to 3 rupees (3 to 5 shillings) per thousand *çlokas* (of 32 syllables). As a specimen of the style of writing to be expected from Benares scribes, the wellwritten MS. of the Khaṇḍanoddhāra-ṭīkā in my collection (see under *Darçana*, p. 44), obtained from the same Pandit, may be noted. The MSS. in question are chiefly old copies of philosophical works. Following the example of Dr F. Hall in his Bibliographical Index, I mention the date in every case where I observed it, as it may be of value in fixing the age of the commentary-literature, much of which is of course of recent, and indeed contemporary, origin.

(1)   A commentary by Çaṅkara Miçra on the Khaṇḍana-khaṇḍa-khādya, a work which, like the Sarvadarçanasaṅgraha, reviews the different schools of Indian philosophy. Commentaries on this work appear to be very rare. The only mention I can find of it is in the Index of Hall, who had heard of it but had not seen it.

The remaining works are chiefly of the Nyāya and Vaiçeshika schools.

(2)   Nyāyavārttika. A portion of this work will shortly be printed by Pandit Vindhyeçварīprasād at Benares. A copy of this MS. is ready.

(3)   Part of Vācaspati Miçra's Nyāyavārttika-tātparya, the Pramāṇa-lakshaṇa, about a quarter of the whole. Dated Lakshmaṇa Saṃvat 417 (A.D. 1523).

(4)   Nyāyakandalī. Copied from a MS. dated Saṃv. 54 of Kashmir. This work appears to be unknown.

(5)   Guṇaprakāçavivṛiti by Bhagīratha. Dated (in words) Çaka 1521 (A.D. 1599).

Amongst MSS. in private possession I may mention two that I noted in one of the lists of books in the Bāla Sarasvati Library (see above p. 25) during the very short time I was there, because the MSS. here, as stated above, are not in all cases given to the Library, though copies can be had.

(6)   A commentary on the Caraṇavyūha.

(7)   A *dīpikā* on the *ṭīkā* of the Hastāmalaka.

(1) A commentary by Gautama Miśra on the Khaṇḍana-khaṇḍakhādya, a work which ... the different schools of Indian philosophy. Copies of this work appear to be very rare. The only mention I can find of it is in the Index of HH, who had heard of it but had not seen it.

The remaining works are chiefly of the Nyāya and Vaiśeṣika schools.

(2) Nyāyacitta. A portion of this work will shortly be printed by Pandit Vindhyeśvariprasād at Benares. A copy of this MS is ready.

(3) ... of Veṅkaṭa. Nyāyakutūhala, being the Pramāṇa section, about a quarter of the whole. Dated Śalimana Samvat 417 (A.D. 1822).

(4) Nyāyatattva. Copied from a MS dated Samvat 3, of Kaśmīr. This work appears to be unknown.

(5) (Nirupakṣavṛtti by Bhagiratha. Dated in words) Śaka 1521 (A.D. 1600).

Amongst MSS in private possession I may mention two that I noted in one of the list of books in the Bāla Sarasvatī Library (see above p. 25) during the very short time I was there, beside the MSS here enumerated above are not in all cases given to the Library, though copies can be had.

(6) A commentary on the Caraṇavyūha.
(7) A digest on the law of the Haribhakta.

APPENDICES.

APPENDIX I.

INSCRIPTIONS.

Table.

I.   At Bhātgāon, Nepal; dated [Gupta] Saṃvat 318 (A.D. 637).

II.   At Patan, Nepal; dated [Çrī-Harsha] Saṃvat 34 (A.D. 640).

III.   ,,   ,,   ,,   ,,   ,,   82 (A.D. 688).

IV.   At Kathmandu, Nepal   ,,   ,,   151 (A.D. 757).

V.   At Patan   ,,   [Nepal] Saṃvat 203 (A.D. 1083).

VI.   ,,   ,,   ,,   ,,   259 (A.D. 1139).

VII.   At Amber, Rajputana; Saṃvat 1011

VIII.   At Aṛ, Mewar; (x—xith cent.).

IX.   Patan, Nepal; Nepal Saṃvat 512 (A.D. 1392).

It will be seen from the above list that the present series affords a more continuous representation of the progress of writing on stone in Nepal than has hitherto been published, which of course gives an interesting parallel to the palæography of the MSS. in our library already described by me. The phraseology, technical terms etc. correspond closely with the published series. See *Indian Antiquary,* IX. 168 sqq., and XIV. 342.

In some of the earlier inscriptions chronological points of considerable importance will be found.

The transcripts now given are prepared from squeezes made by myself on the spot, and in some cases also from photographs made by me from the stone. I have also received some additional squeezes of a few of the Nepal series from Pandit Indrānand. Much still remains undeciphered which probably a second visit to the places might enable me to determine, and something

72 INSCRIPTIONS, NO. I. [APPENDIX I.

further, no doubt, might here and there be got out of my present materials. But, as I have said already, the pressure of other work and want of leisure by daylight renders it undesirable to delay publication.

I. Slab of stone, 18 inches wide, at Golmādhi-ṭol, Bhātgāon. Dated [Gupta-] saṃvat 316 or 318 (A.D. 635-7).

For further particulars see above p. 13 and add a reference to the article on Nepalese chronology in the *Indian Antiquary* for Dec. 1885 (p. 342), where Mr Fleet notes that this inscription 'supplies the keynote' to the interpretation of the early series. As to the units' figure which at p. 13 I have given as 8 I am somewhat uncertain. The symbol, which seems to me to be a numeral-figure and not an *akshara* or letter-numeral like the others, resembles most nearly the 6 in our most archaic Nepalese MS., Add. 1702 (see the table in my Catalogue), though there also 8 is very similar.

[1] स्वस्ति मानगृहादपरिमितगुणसमुदयोद्भा[स्वितदि]-
श्री ब-

[2] प्पपादानुद्ध्यातो लिच्छविकुलकेतुर्भट्टारकमहारा-
जश्रीशिवदे-

[3] वः कुशली माखोष्टंसत्सरद्रङ्गनिवासिनः प्रधान-
[जनपुर]स्तरा-

[4] न्यामकुटुम्बिनः कुशलपरिप्रश्नपूर्व्वं समाज्ञाप[यति]
विदि-

[5] तम्भवतु भवतां यथानेन प्रख्या[तामल]विपुल − − −
− − प

[6] राक्रमोपशमितामितविपच्चप्रभावेन महासामन्तां-
शुएवर्म्म-

[7] णा विज्ञापितेन मयैतद्गौरवाद्युष्मदनुकम्पया च कूबेर्व्व-

VIII

INSCRIPTION NO. 1.

Photographed by the Author.

[8] त्यधिष्ठितानामत्र समुचितखिकरमात्रसाधनाथैव प्रवे-

[9] श्री लिख्यदानपञ्चापराधाद्यत्येन्वप्रवेश[1] इति प्र-
सादी व:

[10] क्रतस्तदेवंवेदिभिरस्त्रप्रसादीपजीविविभिरन्यैर्वा न

[11] कैश्चिद्यमन्यथाकरणीयो यख्तामाज्ञां विलङ्घ्या-
न्यथा कु-

[12] र्योत्कारयेद्वा तमहमतितरान्न मर्षयिय्यामि ये
वास्मदू-

[13] र्ध्वम्भूभुजो भवितारस्तिरपि धर्म्मगुरुभिर्म[ꞏ ꞏ द्द]-
तप्रसा-

[14] दानुवर्तिभिरियमाज्ञा सम्यक्परिपालनीयेति समा-
ज्ञापना

[15] दूतकश्चात्र भोगवर्म्मा स्वामी (*sic*) संवत् २१६ ज्यैष्ठ-
ष्ठउक्कदिवा दशम्याम्

Translation.

Hail ! From Mānagriha.　The illustrious Çivadeva, meditating on the feet of Bappa, who has illuminated the quarters by the dayspring of his countless virtues, being in good health, to the cultivators resident in the villages of Mākhoshṭam and Satsaradraṅga (?) under the lead of their headmen, with due enquiries after their health, addresses the following order :—

"Be it known to you that, at the request of the great

---

[1] *I.e.* apparently, not for purposes of criminal or corrective procedure.　This usage of apraveça seems to throw some light on the form and meaning of the Prakrit apāvesa in the inscription in the Pandulena cave No. 3, as to which Pandit Bhagvānlāl in his learned article in the Bombay Gazetteer (s.v. Nasik) expresses doubt.

feudatory Aṃçuvarman, who by his renowned...doughty and ...prowess has subdued the might of his innumerable foes, out of regard for him and compassion for you, I grant you this boon, namely that the officials of Kūbervatī[1] are allowed entrance for the levying only of not more than the three taxes, but not for granting writings or for the five offences and the like[2]. Therefore this boon must not be infringed by our dependants who have cognisance of this, nor by any other parties whatsoever: and whosoever, in contravention of this order, does so infringe or cause infringement, him I will in no wise suffer; moreover such kings as shall be after us, ought, as guardians of religion and (thus) as followers of grants (made...), to preserve my order in its entirety. In this matter the executive officer is Bhogavarman Svāmin. Saṃvat 316, on the 10th of the bright fortnight of Jyeshṭha."

II. Slab of stone, 14 inches wide, in a place called Sundhārā[3], Patan, Nepal; dated [Çrī-Harsha] Saṃvat 34 (A.D. 640). See pp. 7—8 above.

Doubtful readings are indicated by dots placed under the letters.

1. ‑‑ कैला[स]कूटभवनाद्भगवत्यंशुपति

2.   बप्पपादानुध्यातः श्री म[हा]सा[मन्तांशुवर्म्मा]

3. ‑‑ वर्तमानभविष्यतो

4. समाज्ञपयति विदित[मस्तु] भवताम ‑ ‑

5. ‑ ‑ नृपकुलमथ विनिपतितेष्टकापाङ्क्त्रिविवरप्रविष्ट

---

[1] Qu. 'treasury-officers,' in spite of the somewhat barbarized form.

[2] The five great offences generally enumerated by writers on law and called by them *mahāpātakas* are: (1) murder of a Brahman, (2) theft, (3) adultery with a *guru's* wife, (4) drinking spirituous liquors, (5) intercourse with such as commit these offences. See Manu xi. 55, Vishṇu xxxv. 1—2, Yajñavalkya iii. 227. Dr D. Wright, on the authority (as he informs me) of Pandit Guṇānand only, gives a different list at p. 189 of his History.

[3] This must be the stone referred to by Dr D. Wright in his History p. 246, note. Yet I should hardly call the inscription 'effaced,' though the part above the present level of the street is much worn.

IX

INSCRIPTION NO. II.

Photographed by the Author.

6.　नकुलकुलाकुलितमूषिक – – पुर विघटित निरव

7.　षद्द्वारकवाटवातायनादिजीर्णदारुसंघातं यत्नतः

8.　प्रतिसंस्कार्य तस्य दीर्घतरपश्चात्कालसौस्थित्यनिमित्त

9.　[म]चयनीविप्रतिबद्धमेवं माटिङ्ग्रामस्य दक्षिणतो राज-

10.　भोग्यतामापन्नं विंशतिकय – – षष्टिमानिकपिण्डकां[1] चि

11.　चम् दक्षिणपश्चिमतस्स्रष्षण्मानिकापिण्डकम्माटिङ्ग्रामपा

12.　ञ्चालिकेभ्यः प्रतिपादितमेवंविदिभिर्न कैश्चिदस्मत्पाद

13.　प्रतिबद्धजीवनैरन्यैर्वायन्न मे धिकारी न्यथा करणीय[:।]

14.　यस्त्वेतामाज्ञामुल्लङ्घ्यान्यथा कुर्यात्कारयेद्वा तं वयन्न मा[र्ष]

15.　यिष्यामो भवष्यिद्भिरपि भूपतिभिर्धर्मगुरुभिर्धर्माधि

16.　कारप्रतिपालनादू तैर्भवितव्यम् संवत् ३४ प्रथमपौष

17.　मुक्लद्वितीयायाम् [दू]तकोऽत्र महाबलाध्यक्षविन्दुस्वामी॥

Translation.

From the palace of Kailāsakūṭa [the sovereign[2]] who
meditates on the feet of Bappa addresses the following order
to the present and future [officials of certain places]: "Be it
known to you that...the royal family: now that I have
diligently had replaced the mass of decayed wood belonging to
the doors, panels, windows etc., which have been entirely
destroyed, since the crevices in the layers of bricks that have
fallen away have been entered by tribes of ichneumons who

---

[1] Read पिण्डकं

[2] The name of the great feudatory Aṃçuvarman may be restored with
tolerable certainty. Compare the last inscription and number 6 in Pandit
Bhagvānlāl's series dating from the same year.

worried the mice [already there], to ensure its good condition for the longer time to come, there has been thus attached as an endowment a field to the south of the village of Mātiṅ, heretofore included in the crown-estate, measuring 20 [measures and producing] the revenue of 60 *mās*; and to the south-west one producing the revenue of 6 *mās* is handed over to the Pāñcālikas of the village of Mātiṅ. My authority herein must not be infringed [etc., as in other inscriptions of Aṃçuvarman]. Saṃvat 34, on the second day of the light half of the first (intercalary) Pausha. My appointed agent herein is Vindusvāmin, chief Minister of War."

The most important point in this inscription is the intercalation occurring in the date. My surmise that an intercalation was referred to in the expression *prathama* was first confirmed by Mr Fleet, to whom I showed my reading, but Professor Bühler of Vienna, to whom I am indebted for much help in deciphering this and the following inscription, called my attention to its great importance. Dr Bühler also kindly submitted the date to the examination of Dr Schram, Privatdocent für chronologische Astronomie at the Vienna University, from whom I have received through Dr Bühler some very elaborate and valuable calculations. I think it would be beyond the scope of the present publication to reproduce these here, but my obligation is none the less. Professor Adams has also most kindly worked out the calculations. From these two eminent authorities I have obtained the following results : (1) that the Nepalese at the time of the inscription used as the basis of their calendar not the Sūryasiddhānta (in which Pausha is never intercalary, it would seem), but a work that had the same elements as the Brahmasiddhānta; (2) that the year 640 A.D. according to this rule is intercalary, which adds another confirmation, if any be needed, to the theory that the era of this group of inscriptions is that of Çrī-Harsha (A.D. 606).

III.   Slab of stone, 15 inches wide, at Gairi-dhārā, Patan, Nepal.   Dated [Çrī-Harsha] Saṃvat 82 (A.D. 688).

1. [स्व]ास्ति]कैलासकूट[भ]वना[द]
      ....

2.

3.

4.

5.

6.

7.   तप

8.   ले भगवद्वज्रेश्वर प्रण
        ...   .

9. — — — — — सर्वाधिकरण ना मप्रविधातव्य नृप
                              ...   .

10. — — — — — गण प्रसादीकृतमनेनाथ — — न्तु
        ....

11. — — नात्मनः श्रेयोभिवृद्धये धार्मिकगणनमतिसृष्टम्

12. प्रतिपालन प्रतिज्ञा न यो ग कर्म यो गुर
          ....

13.   ि— — — कालमनतिक्रम्य प्रधानम्
                                    ....

14. — — — गन्धपुष्पधूपप्रदीपवर्षवर्धनवर्षाकाल
                    ...   .

15. — — मन्त्रजपकादिप्रकरणपूजा कर्तव्या पाश्चाल्याच्च
                ...   ...

16. उपलिपनसम्मार्जनप्रतिसंस्काराादिकं कृत्वा यद्यस्ति
                          ... ...

17. परिशेषन्तेन द्रव्येण भगवन्तं वज्रेश्वरमुद्दिश्य

18. पाशुपतानाम्ब्राह्मणानाच्च यथासम्भवम्भोजनङ्कर

19. णीयन्तदन्यच्च कालान्तरेण यदि कदाचिद्दानपति

20. बिन प्रार्थयन्त आपत्सु तत्कालम्बुध्वा दानपतीनाम्

21. धान्यानाच्चतुर्विंशतिमानिका देया अतोधिकन्[द]ानप

22. तिभिने ग्राह्यं यदा चाच कार्य्यमुत्पद्यते परमासन

23. [म]धिकारमाच्चङ्करणीयन्न तु द्रव्यस्याचेपस्तदेव

24. [म]वगत सर्व्वाधिकरणाधिक्षतैर्न्यैवा न कश्चिदयम्[1]

25. अस्मत्प्रसादीन्यथा कर्त्तव्यो येल्सदाज्ञां व्यतिक्रम्यवर्त[न्ते]

26. वयन्तेषान्न मर्षयामो ये य्स्मदूर्ध्वेम्भवितारी राजा

27. नस्तैरपि पर्वनृपतिक्षतप्रसादप्रतिपालनादृ

28. तैनान्यथा करणीयं खयमाज्ञा दूतकश्चाच भट्टार

29. [क]युवराज स्कन्ददेव: संवत् ट२ [भाद्र] पद ४उ४ दि

30. − − म् ॥   ॥

Translation.

From the palace of Kailāsakūṭa……………………………………
(ll. 11, 12) for [his] own increase of prosperity the enumeration of the righteous[2]…handed over [for] protection[2]…(l. 13) not overstepping the due time, worship must be performed having as its occasion [the offering of] spells charms etc. for [hastening] the rainy season and for increasing rain[3] and odours, flowers, incense, lights…; and with the Pāñcālī-community, after having done all such business as smearing with cow-dung, cleansing and repairs, if a residue remains, with that money in honour of the blessed Vajreçvara[4] a feast is to be made, as far as means

<hr>

[1] Read कैश्चिद॰

[2] These phrases cannot be translated with any certainty without more context. *Dhārmikagaṇanam* is perhaps to be compared with *Guṇigaṇagaṇana* in Pañcatantra, Introd. 8. (=Hitop. Introd. 15). *Atisṛishṭam pratipālanāya* occurs in Bhagvānlāl's Inscr. No. 7, line 14.

[3] A specimen of this class of *pūjā* is the *Megha-sūtra*, edited by me in the R. A. S. Journal for 1880.

[4] 'To gain [a god's] favour', B. and R. s. v. ud-diç. *Vajreçvarī* and

X.

INSCRIPTION NO. III.

A photographic reproduction of part of the back of a paper squeeze.

XI.

1. INSCRIPTION REFERRED TO AT PAGE 14, LINE 8.
2.   „   NO. IV. SEE PAGES 4, 79.
3.   „   NO. VII.   „   29, 81.

From squeezes.

allow, to the Pāçupata ascetics and Brahmans; and in case perchance on another occasion, on the strength of their being benefactors, people ask for something else than this, in times of need, then, after you have ascertained that this is the proper time for it, 24 *mānikās* of grain may be given to benefactors; more than this is not to be taken by the benefactors. Now when a law-suit arises[1] as to these points, the Supreme Court is to be constituted the standard (?) of authority[2]; but the money must not be thrown away. With this understanding neither the fully authorised officer nor any other parties whatsoever may controvert this boon, (etc., as in the other inscriptions).

Our appointed agent in this matter is the heir apparent Skandadeva[3]. Saṃvat 82, Bhādrapada, bright half…

IV. Water-conduit slab near the temple of Jaisi, Kathmandu. Dated [Çrī-Harsha] Saṃvat 151 (A.D. 757). See p. 4, above.

1. ॐ संवत् १५१ वैशाख शुक्ल द्वितीयायाम्

2. लच्छ्मव्ल्याञ्चाकाय[ा]न्वित्योपभोगार्थम्

3. अतीतलब्धस्य भार्याया[4] भीजमत्या दत्तम्

4. जलद्रोणिन सह – – मा २॥ ॥

Vajrapāṇi are Buddhist divinities; and as the *vajra* is very rarely Sivaic, while Vaishnavism is very little known in Nepal, it seems fair to infer that we find here early traces of the curious juxtaposition of Hindu and Buddhist cult that the Tantric system brought into Nepal.

[1] Cf. Manu 8. 43.

[2] The exact force of *mātra* is not easy to express. It cannot well have its common meaning 'merely'; if it does not convey anything of its radical meaning of measure, as suggested above, it probably serves only to give slight additional definition or emphasis to *adhikāra*.

[3] I could not discern any remains of the *k* on the stone but *s* (conjunct) and *nd* were fairly distinct; and, though not clear in the squeeze from which the autotype has been prepared, in another squeeze made by me the *n* conjunct comes out very well and the *s* and *d* very fairly. Observe that the *d* is written *below* in the conjunct न्द in Gupta writing. The (*akshara*) form of 80 is also much clearer in this squeeze. I am not sure whether the unit-figure is 2 or 3.

[4] Read भार्यया.

"Saṃvat 151, on the second day of the light half of Vaiçākha, Bhojamati wife of Atītalambha gave two mās [of land?] to the Pañch-committee of Lañjagval, together with a water-receptacle, for their perpetual enjoyment thereof."

What *jaladroṇa* may mean precisely I have no means of telling; and the dictionaries give no help. I at first thought from the position of the stone and from a possible connexion with √dru 'run' that it must mean water-*course*, like *praṇāli*: but the ordinary meaning of *droṇa*, 'tub', rather suggests a reservoir; and to this view Dr Bühler, I find, is inclined. The word *droṇa* occurs also in the next inscription, and there the first meaning is perhaps more probable. The gradual approximation to Kuṭila forms in the characters of this inscription is noticeable, particularly in the lengthened and more sweeping *curves* of medial *ā* and *ī*.

V. Dedicatory verses on the pedestal of a figure of the sun-god, Patan, Nepal. Dated [Nepal] Samvat 203 (A.D. 1083). See pp. 8–9 with plate. Space covered by inscription, $5\frac{1}{2} \times 2\frac{3}{4}$ inches.

1. ७ त्रिभिर्वर्षैः समायुक्ते संवत्सरशतदये । वैशाखशु

2. क्लशप्तम्यां [sic] बुधे पुष्योदये श्डुभा [॥] श्रीयशोदेवभूनाथत

3. नयो धर्मतत्पर: । श्रीवाणदेव: कृतवान् प्रतिमां सु

4. प्रतिष्ठितां । दिवाकरस्य या माचा पुरा संकल्पिता मुदा

5. कर्तुस्तिनास्तु सततं तेजोवृद्धिरनुत्तरा ॥ ० ॥

Translation.

When two hundred years were joined with three, on the 7th of the bright half of Vaiçākha, on Wednesday, Pushyā was auspicious at its rising. Vāṇadeva son of king Yaçodeva, religiously disposed, made [this] image well set up in honour of the Sun, which had previously been planned by his mother with

XII

INSCRIPTION NO. VI.

From a squeeze.

ʻrejoicing. Therefore to the maker may there ever accrue supreme increase of glory!

It is interesting to compare the forms of the letters of Add. 1684 in our library (*Catal.* pp. xxv. 173 and Table of Letters) with those of this inscription.

VI. Inscription of Mānadeva's reign, dated Nepal Saṃvat 259 (A.D. 1139). See p. 10 above.

१ सम्वत् २५९ भाद्रपद कृष्ण सप्तम्यां । श्रीमत्

राजाधिराज परमेश्वर (2) परमभट्टारक । श्रीमानदेवस्य वि-

जयराज्ये । श्री दनीश्व[र]दक्षिण धिवा (3) सिन । दिवंश्रत-

पजनवननिर्मितेन तच्चैव । यौ धिवासिन । द्रौनमेव (4) नद्या:

तत पन्नालि कर्त्तव्यम् नित्यवच्छिन्नन् सम्प्रदत्तं

This inscription is reproduced only on account of its date and style of writing. One might well suppose it to have been scratched on the stone by a second-rate MS. copyist, for both the incision and the attempt at Sanskrit are unusually feeble for an inscription of such a date; so much so that I have not attempted a translation. It records the gift of a water-channel (*pannāli* of course for *praṇāli*) and a *droṇa* (see last inscription).

The great interest of the discovery is that we find here an instance, unique as far as I know, of the use of the peculiar local *hooked hand* of Nepal which has been abundantly illustrated in the Palæographical Society's Oriental Series as well as in my Catalogue.

This and the preceding inscription thus form a link, in point of character, between the periods illustrated by Nos. 1—15 and that of Nos. 16, 17, etc. in Pandit Bhagvānlāl's series.

VII. Tablet in the wall of a temple on a hill above Amber, Rajputana. Date Saṃvat 1011 = A.D. 954, if, as supposed at p. 29 above, the Vikrama era be used.

<table>
<tr><td>संवत १०११ भाद्रपदे ब</td><td>— भु — द</td></tr>
<tr><td>दि ११ सुक्र दिन ज — — तन</td><td>रीसुतः</td></tr>
<tr><td></td><td>व्रददात्</td></tr>
</table>

VIII.   Fragment built into a staircase at Aṛ, near Oodeypore (Mewar).   Width of inscription 3 feet 6 inches.   See p. 32.

1.   — न्वटी चपटलाधिपृतिः समेतः कारंडिकैः सदर्सि ग्रक्तिकुमारमेव । विज्ञप्तवान्सकलधर्म्मविधानविज्ञः प्रज्ञाप्रकर्ष- चतुरी नृपतिं वचोभिः ॥ द्रम्मानष्ट लभामहै चितिप यान्षट्- चक्रमा ह्रीमदाघाटम

2.   — युक्तकरण्ड — भ — के ब्दं प्रति । ते स्माभिश्वतुर्दंग्रापि तपनायास्मै प्रदत्ता इति श्रुवा तेन महीभृता ख्वचनेनैते ख्दत्ताः कृताः ॥ ग्ररीरं जीवितं लच्मीः सर्वं ज्ञात्वेत्यसास्वतं । भानवे मी प्रदातव्या द्रम्मा भाविनि ये

Translation.

—nnaṭa, the record-keeper[1], attended by the casket bearers (?)[2], in conclave reported to the King, even Çaktikumāra (discerning was he in the ordering of every law and skilled in the pre-eminence of prudence) in these words: "Let us take eight drachms, my liege, which up to the six-fold circle......[offer in] suitable caskets year by year. These fourteen, however, we have offered to yonder sun." When the King heard this he made a free gift of these...by his own word, saying: "We know that body, life, our fortune, all are an unconstant thing: so these drachms are to be offered to the Sun, O lady..."

---

[1] For *akshapatalādhipati* compare the inscriptions in the *Indian Antiquary* for 1877, pp. 196, 200.

[2] This is a mere guess, for *kāraṇḍika* is not to be found in dictionaries.

INSCRIPTION NO. VIII.

From a squeeze.

IX. Slab of slate in the courtyard of the temple of Kumbheçvara, Patan, Nepal; dated Nepal Saṃvat 512 (A.D. 1392).

Size of inscribed portion of slab, 1 ft. 4½ in. × 1 ft. 3½ in. Facsimile photographed from my heelball rubbing; see p. 12.

1. स्वस्ति श्रीमन्निपलिक सम्वत् ५१२ वैशाखकृष्णषष्ठ्यां तिथौ ॥ घरकरणि[1] । विखमुहूर्त्ते

2. श्रवणनच्चें । ऐन्द्रयोगे । आदित्य वाश्ररे ॥ श्रीललितपत्तननगरोत्तमे ॥ श्रीश्रीम[न्न]

3. [हा]कुमारसप्तफणावलीमणिकिरणसंद्योतायमान श्रीनागराजाधिष्ठिते ॥ परमेश्वरपरम

4. भट्टारक श्रीमानेश्वरीवरलब्धप्रसाद असुरनारायणेत्यादि विविधविरुदराजावलीपूर्व्व-

5. – – – – क्रियासमालंकृत महाराजाधिराज श्रीश्रीमत् जयस्थिति राज मल्लदेवेन संभुज्यमान

6. [राज्ये] ॥ ॥ श्रीमत्सप्तकुटुम्बजप्रधानमूर्त्यंग महायाच श्रीविभयाचप्रमुखादिभिः संयाट

7. – ने । श्रीमानीगलोत्तरस्थाने । अस्ति तच्च महातीर्थः कुंभतीर्थं इति ख्यतः । यच्चैष भग-

वान्देवः श्री-

8. [कुं]भेश्वरशंकरः । तस्याग्रियदिग्ग्रि स्थाने विघ्नराजश्च वाश्रुकी । दच्चिणे मातरः सर्वाः पिढतीर्थस्त

[1] This must be the Hindustani سرکرنی.

9. [दुत्त]रे । वायव्या चैव दिग्भागे गौरी पुष्करिणी च ते । ऐशान्यां केशवश्चैवं मध्ये कुंभेश्वर:

10. शिव: ॥ कुंभर्षिमुनिमुख्येन पत्नी ‑ पि तप: कृतं । आराधितो महादेवस्तेन कुंभे-

11. श्वर: स्तत: ॥ पुष्करिण्या च यत्तीये य: करोत्यवगाहनं । श्रावणे पूर्णिमास्यां वै सो पि स्वर्ग-

12. [स्वा]भुयात् ॥ यत्पादाम्बुजसंपूतं निर्मलदूरितापदं । प्रणालिकमुखद्वारान्तीयं वहति

13. [नित्]यग्र: । यत्तीर्यांड्डवववारिणा सुनियतं स्नात्वा नरो नित्यग्र: पीत्वा वारि सुनिर्म्मितं
किमथवा कृत्वा

14. मुखचालनं । नित्यं यो यभिवन्दते प्रतिदिनं श्रीदेवकुम्भेश्वरं भुक्त्वा सर्वसुखानि याति नगरीं सों-

15. ते पुरां ग्राम्भवी बभूव तत्र कुम्भेग्र: प्रासादरहित: परं । आवासमाचमंच्छन्न स्थित: कुम्भेश्वर:

16. शिव: । अस्ति पुण्याद्धि संभूतो जयभीमो नरोत्तम: । पाङिंसिंकी गृहस्थाने समावासी धनेश्वर:

17. ॥ परोपकर्व्यवग्रायग्रीलो दाता गुणज्ञो हि विवेकी । पुचोत्तमो यं गुणवर्म्मणो ऽसौ साचा

18. त् हरिश्चन्द्र द्वेष धीर: । तस्यांगना महाग्रीला अनन्तलच्छी विश्रुता । पीडिताज्वरभोगेन मुमू

19. र्छे ग्रयने च सा । तां जीवयितुं प्राड्योऽसौ जयभीमो विचच्चण: कुंभेश्वरालयं कर्त्तुं प्रतिज्ञा छ

INSCRIPTION NO. IX.

From a heelball rubbing.

20. तवांस्तत: ॥ न रचिता तथायेवं नीता खर्गं शिवेन सा । खां वाचं प्रतिरचार्थं करोति स शिवालयं

21. ॥ दितीया अभयलच्मी च अभयदेव सुतस्तथा ॥ जयतेजो नुजस्तस्य तेषां सुसंमतेन च ॥ क्वा दे

22. वालयं रम्यं प्रासादं हि सतोरणं विप्रोधीकृत्य भूमिं च प्राकारै: परिवेष्टितं । क्वा चातुर्म्मुखं

23. कीग्रं सौवर्णं रत्नमण्डितं । ढि:किणी¹ सुविचिचां च ढींकिला परमेश्वरं । क्वा लचाह्रतिं तस्मिन् वेद

24. घोषै सुमंगलं । समारोपितवांस्तच्च सुवर्णकलसध्वजं । अनेन क्रतपुण्ठिन चातुर्वर्ष्यॊदयो ज

25. ना: । प्राम्नुवंतु महासौख्यमंते च परमम्पदं । येनाकारि महेश्वरस्य भवनं विष्णोस्तथान्यस्य वा तस्मि

26. न् काष्ठम्लेष्ठकं निपतितं कुर्व्वेति ये स्थापनं । तेषामेव सुखं भवत्यनुदिनं भूत्वा धनाढ्यं नरास्ते

27. न्ते यान्ति पुरीं शिवस्य नगरीं मोदन्ति तस्मिन्सदा ॥ श्रुभं भवतु सर्व्वेषां शिवं भवतु सर्व्विदा: ॥ ✳ ॥

¹ Apparently a form of the Hindi ढकनी

Translation (see also abstract at p. 12).

Hail! In the year of Nepal 512, on the 6th lunar day of the dark half of Vaiçākha.

By order of Government. In the Çravaṇa asterism and the Aindra conjunction, Sunday.

In the capital city Lalita-pattana, presided over by the snake-king who is glorious with the rays of the gems of his cluster of seven hoods, the sovereignty being enjoyed by Jayasthiti the sovereign lord, who has gained favour from the bounty of Māneçvarī, whose royal lineage...[is renowned]...in various panegyrics as of the Asuras and Nārāyaṇa, who is adorned by [?mighty] deeds. In the northern region of Mānīgala[1], there is the great *tirth* called Kumbhatīrtha, where lives this venerable God Kumbheçvara[2]. On the south-east side are Gaṇeça and Vāçukī, on the south all the divine Mothers, the *tirth* of the Fathers is to the north, in the north-west quarter are Gaurī and Pushkariṇī in the north-east likewise Vishṇu, and in the centre Kumbheçvara. With Agastya the sage born in the *kumbha* (pitcher) at the head...penance is done: by him Mahādeva is worshipped, and hence called Kumbheçvara, and with the water of the lake whoso makes ablution at the full moon of Çrāvaṇa, even he can obtain heaven.

Cleansed by the lotus of his feet and void of spot, stain or evil, from the mouthpiece of a conduit the water flows perpetually.

With the water from this *tīrth* if a man has strictly washed, and regularly drunk the water well meted out and has performed the rinsing of the mouth, or whoso daily and constantly salutes Kumbheçvara, he enjoys all pleasures and goes at last to the city and town of Çiva. At that place was Çiva destitute of a temple thereupon: Çiva Kumbheçvara abode

---

[1] I omit the previous sentence as being partly obliterated and partly containing names and allusions, probably local, of which I have no knowledge.

[2] As to this form of Çiva we may compare the Ashtamīvrata-vidhāna translated by Wilson (Essays, ed. Rost, ii. 32), from which it will be seen that the cult referred to here is of the Tantric school.

under the mere shelter of a dwelling-house.   [For the contents
of lines 16—23 see p. 12].

(Line 23.)   He has also made a variegated cover [for the
treasury or treasure-case] approaching the mighty Lord, making
thereon an offering of a lac auspicious with sounds of [recitations
from ?] the Veda : there too he has erected a golden pinnacle and
banner.   Through him, the doer of such a good work, may the
people sprung from the four castes[1] attain great bliss and a
mansion in the highest at the last ! The man who makes a
dwelling for Çiva and also Vishṇu or some other deity, to him
is allotted wood, stone and brick.   Such men as set up [the
image of a god], to them accrues blessing, day by day becoming
riches : those men go to Çiva's city and delight in it for ever.

[1] Read °*odayā* and understand of the Hindus proper as opposed to Buddhists
and aborigines.

APPENDIX II.

ROUGH LIST OF MSS. IN THE LIBRARY OF THE JAIN MANDIR AT RĀMGHĀṬ, BENARES.

The following list is transcribed into Roman characters from a copy kindly made for my use, as mentioned at p. 24 above. I give it in the form I received it, only correcting a few obvious mistakes and not attempting to reconstruct the names of the less known works. It will be noted that the collection includes several of the Brahmanical works, (such as the poems of Kālidāsa) often found in Jain libraries, as well as numerous tracts in the vernaculars, as to which I have little knowledge.

No. of library case.		No. of leaves.	No. of library-case.		No. of leaves.
1.	Bhagavatī-vṛitti	626		Sādhupratikramaṇa-bālabodha	10
	Bhagavatī-sūtra	324		Guṇasthānakramaroha-mūla	15
3.	Uttarādhyayana	360	5.	Hemī Nāmamālā	102
	Dīpotsava-vyākhyāna	20		Ācārāṅga	96
	Uvavāī-ṭabbā	99		Paṇṇāvaṇā	340
	Jñātādharma-vṛitti	74		Kumārasambhava-kāvya	20
	Pariçishṭa-parvan	111		Antagaḍadaçā	11
	Sūyagaḍānga	45		Nirayāvalī	39
	Pañca-saṅgraha	39		Upadeçamālā	
	Saṃyaktvakaumudī	35		Gajasiṃha-carita	125
4.	Ṭhānāṅga	78		Çilopadeçamālā	104
	Chaitri-pūnima-vyā-khyāna (?)	3	6.	Kalpadrumakulika	182
	Jñātā [dharma]-sūtra-ṭabba	317		Ashṭābdhi-kāvyākhyāna	12
	Nirayāvalī-sūtra-ṭabba	73		Kalpasūtra	75
	Upāsakadaçā	57		Daçamīkalikā (? vaikāl°)	38
	Rāyapaseṇīpañcapāta(?)	110		Tarkabhāshā	23

No. of library-case.		No. of leaves.
	Tarkasaṅgrahasamagra	1
	Kalpa-kir[a]ṇāvalī	229
	Bhartṛihari-prathama-dvitīyaçataka-ṭīka	37
	Bhartṛihari-tritīya	17
	Dharmapāṭha	62
7.	Çrīpalacopäī [Hindi]	29
	Vipākasūtra	74
	Prathamakrama-grantha sūtra	25
	Çrāddha-vidhi	42
	Saṅgrahaṇī-vṛitti	98
	Uttarādhyayana	267
8.	Uvasaggahara-ṭīkā	9
	Ashṭādhyāyī	38
	Aniṭ-akārikā-tripāṭa	6
	Sārasvata (uttarārddha)	42
	Amaradattamitrananda rāsa	40
	Vasūpūjyasvāmi-rāsa	22
	Nala-Davadantī-copäī	38
	Kaya-valhā (?) copäī	18
	Copolī-copäī	11
	Rātribhojana-copäī	15
	Caṃdarāsa	72
	Gāthāsahasrī	40
	Kālagrahaṇāvidhī	15
	Vicāra-çataka	38
	Varshatantra-ṭīkā	36
	Nāracandra prathama prakaraṇa	19
	Dvādaçabhāvaphalam	9
	J[y]otisha-ṭīkā	8
	Sindūraprakaraṇa	30
	Dānaçīla-codhāliyo	9
9.	Pañcakarma-grantha-yantra	56
	Gautama-pṛicchā	53

No. of library-case.		No. of leaves.
	Meru-trayodaçī-vyākhyāna	11
	Munipati-caritra gadya	52
	Nigoda-chabīçī-satīkā	7
	Caüsaraṇa-painṇā-ṭabbā	7
	Nīlakaṇṭha-tājikā	26
	Sārasvata	63
10.	Rasacandrikā	24
	Vāgbhaṭa-alaṅkāra	8
	Sūryaprajñapti	98
	Dṛishṭāntaçataka-ṭabbā	19
	Vaiyākaraṇa-bhūshaṇa	35
	Sandehaviçodhi	51
	Sadbhāshitāvalī	14
	Haima-çabdānuçāsana	11
	Samarasāra-ṭīkā	14
	Sāmudraka	13
	Comm. on part of Madhava's Nidāna	11
	Vaidyavinoda	18
	Sūtra çṛiṅgāra (?)	5
	Bālavicāra (?) dharma ke phuṭhakaro (?)	20
11.	Shaḍdarçanasamuccaya-ṭīkā	75
	Caṅdapaññatti-ṭīkā	199
	Sūyapaññatti-sūtra.	94
	Yogaçāstradīpikā	253
12.	Siddhānta-candrikā	116
	Sārasvata-ṭīkā Mādhavī	117
	Prabodhacandrikā	20
13.	Mahīpālacaritra prākṛita-gāthā vadha (?)	51
	Saṃvapradyuna rāsarakhaṃda (??)	17
	Mṛigāvalī rāsa	27
	Karmagrantha 4 bālabodha	115

No. of library-case.		No. of leaves.	No. of library-case.		No. of leaves.
	Siddhāṃ[ta]kebolvicāra	27		Nirayāvalī	43
14.	Janmapatra-paddhati	289		Kathākoça-gadya	86
	Laghukaumudī	110	21.	Dhālasāgara	225
	Kalpakaumudī	274		Pārçvanāthacaritra-gadya	79
15.	Jambu-adhyeyana-ṭabbā	63		Praçnavyākaraṇa-ṭabbā	202
	Çāntinātha-caritra-gadya	230	22.	Haima-lingānuçāsana	140
	Çatruñjayamāhātmya-ṭabbā	282		Haima-anekārtha	40
16.	Raghuvaṃça	110		Çabda-ratnākara	26
	Jñānārṇava-padya (?)	124		Vāṇi-bhūshaṇa	23
	Çrīpāla caritra-gadya	33		Pingala	43
	Loka... vritti (?)	8		Rāmavinoda	71
	Ātma-prabodha	137		Sanghayana-bālabodha	71
17.	Guṇa-kramārohavritti	26		Vaidyajīvana	25
	Antagaḍaçā	27	23.	Rāmacaritra-gadya	133
	Navatattva-vicāra-ṭabbā	10		Madanavinoda-nighaṇṭu	89
	Shaḍāvaçyaka-vritti	86		Kautuka-patra	24
	Uttarādhyayana-ṭīkā Nemicandra-kritā	166		Vasantarāja-racita-çākuna-çāstra	137
	Sattarīsaya-gaṇa	29		Madanavinoda-ni-ghaṇṭu	107
	Uvavāī-ṭīka	82	24.	Çakuntalā-nāṭaka	75
18.	Mahādaṇḍaka	30		Sugati paṃkshā (?)	41
	Annadāna-vishaye Bho-jakathā	49		Nīlakaṇṭhajātaka-pad-dhati	46
	Haima-Anekārthasan-graha	70		Jyotisha-ratnamālā	49
19.	Shaṭ karmagranthāḥ [or 'Shaṭ-sūtra']	8		Vedāntasāra	18
	Tarkaparibhāshā	18		Kirātārjunīya-kāvya	108
	Navatattva-bālabodha	158		Kumārasambhava-kāvya	482
	Upadeçamālā-vivaraṇa	77		[Of cases 25—30, 33—4, 36—41 no account.]	
	Kavi-taranga vaidyaka	44	31.	Vipākasūtra-ṭīkā	30
	Jīva[vi]cāra-navatattva-vritti	45		Ratna kalarāsa (?)	91
	Haima-daṇḍaka	27		Hari[ç]cand[r]a-nripa-copaī	53
20.	Paṇṇāvaṇā-vritti	336		Vimala-rāsa	44
	Shaḍāvaçyaka-ṭabbā	33	32.	Mantra-mahodadhi	60
				Çārī[ra]ka-bhāshya	160

No. of library-case.		No. of leaves.	No. of library-case.		No. of leaves.
35.	Uttarādhyayana-vritti	210		Ratnāvalī nātikā	28
	Gacchācāra-païnnā-vritti	140		Daça drishtāntāḥ	30
	Pannāvanā-vritti	249		Sphoṭa-candrikā	16
	Sambo[dha]sattari	55		Jambūdvīpa-paññattī sūtra	108
	Caüsaranā-payannā-tripāṭha-vritti	19		Nemicaritra padya	
	Praçnavyākarana-ṭabbā	108		Ṛishi-maṇḍala-prakaraṇa saṭīka	
42.	Pāṇḍavacaritra	163	47.	Lokaprakāça citra-sahita	452
43.	Pannāvanā-sūtra	108		Vicāraratnākara	186
	Nalacaritra-çloka-baddha (?)	148		Baṅga culiyāe sūya-hīluppakkhī (?) ajjha-yaṇa	10
	Dutāṅgadā-chāyā-nātaka	12		Mahāniçītha-sūtra	95
	Adhyātma-kalpadruma	7		Lalitavistara	44
	Alaṃkāra-mañjarī	6		Aṅgaculiyā sūtra	
44.	Prabodha-cintāmaṇi	46	48.	Sūyagaḍaṃga-dīpikā	55
	Pravacanasāroddhāra-mūla	24		Jātakalpa sūtra	4
	Rāyapaseṇi-pañca-sātha (?)	110		Ammati-sūtra	8
	Nyāyamañjushā-vritti	67		Sukritasāgara	33
	,, -mūla	2		Hemonādiganasūtra-vivaraṇa (?)	33
	Saṅgrahaṇī-ṭīkā	41		Praçnottara-sārddhaça-takabhāshā	34
	Tarkaparibhāshā	13		Syādvāda-mañjarī	
	Jyotisharatnamālā	25	50.	Mānasāgarapaddhati	124
	Nidānajana	12		Jātakatattva	38
	Gāthā-ratna-koça	23		Haimaḍhunḍhi-jainen-dravyākaraṇa Laghu-ṭīkā	132
	Caüsaraṇa-bālabodha	12			
	Nandī-sūtra	22			
45.	Prākritavyākaraṇa	96	51.	Pratyekabuddha-copāï	26
	Tājikasāravritti	79		Ācārāṅga-sūtra	59
	Prākrita-manorama	17		Vastupāla-Tejapāla copāï	34
	Çrīpālacaritra-saṭīka	155		Samavāyāṅga-sūtra	37
46.	Pūjāshṭa-phalavishaye kathā	28		Siṃghāsanabattīsī	75
	Çravaṇa-bhūshaṇa	6		Saṅgrahaṇī-vritti	64
	Nandīçvarastava-vritti	25			
	Rasataraṅgiṇī	17			

APPENDIX III.

Revised Chronological Tables of the kings of Nepal, showing additional dates and particulars gained since the publication of my "Catalogue of Buddhist MSS....with notices...of the chronology of Nepal", chiefly during my visit to the country.

General Addenda to that work, with notices of criticisms.

As the above tables are given by way of supplement to the results tabulated in the Historical Introduction to my Catalogue, I take this opportunity of offering a few remarks on some points touched on in the criticisms[1] that have appeared on that work, and likewise of calling attention to several passages in the work in general, to which my notice has been directed from these and from other sources.

And first as regards the Historical or, as I perhaps might have called it, the Chronological Introduction. Dr Oldenberg thinks that my remarks (Catalogue, p. vi sqq.) on the relation of the dates given in the MSS. to the native chronicles and to the dates given by Kirkpatrick are somewhat infelicitous, in that I had "evidently not at all, or only unconnectedly, made such researches as might have given clear insight into the origin and value of the earlier Nepalese tradition."

I am not at all sure that detailed criticism of the Vamçāvalī would have formed a legitimate part of a library catalogue, the object of which seems to me rather to provide material for research than to originate theories. Be this as it may, the necessity for the critical investigation of the period before 1000 A.D. was to a great extent rendered unnecessary by the promise, to which I referred at p. xli, of a sequel to the article by Drs Bhagvānlāl and Bühler in the *Indian Antiquary* for August 1880. This has now appeared in the same journal for December 1884[2] and deals with the relation of the Vamçāvalī to the inscriptions down to the IXth century, the writers being pleased to consider my treatment of the period covered by the later group of inscriptions so "carefully worked out" as to render further notice unnecessary. This being so, I am still somewhat at a loss,—though I have, I hope, sufficiently pondered on Dr Oldenberg's strictures,—to know what precisely are the available

---

[1] See the *Athenæum* for 15 Sept. 1883 ; *Academy* for 30 August 1884 (vol. 26, p. 140) (Prof. T. W. Rhys Davids) ; *Deutsche Litteraturzeitung*, 22 Dec. 1883 (Dr H. Oldenberg) ; *Göttingische Gelehrte Anzeigen* 18 Sept. 1885 (Prof. Th. Zachariae) ; *Litterarisches Centralblatt* 21 March 1885, [Prof. E.] Wi[ndisch] ; *Journal Asiatique*, Jan. 1886 (M. L. Feer).

[2] The present co-editor, Mr Fleet, has now published another paper on this subject, in the number for December 1885, as noted at p. 72 above.

materials for the critical '*Untersuchungen*' that he would have me institute.

As for documentary material, I have made some use for the present publication of a manuscript of the Vaṃçāvalī, as already stated (page 16, note); but I find that its differences from the text translated by Dr Wright consist almost entirely in the omission of a few of the legendary and anecdotal passages of that work. Some differences, indeed, of assigned lengths of reign there are, and these have been registered in the columns of the Table of Kings (under "Gorkha histories"); but the tradition is clearly the same. As to its value I agree with Pandit Bhagvānlāl that "Dr Wright's data are on the whole trustworthy," and I think that the new matter I have now brought to light tends to give remarkable confirmation of these native records which are not to be so lightly set aside as some critics would have us believe. This applies also to a date (A.D. 1141) noted by me at Paris, in the Hodgson collection of the Bibliothèque Nationale, while passing the present work through the press. Though of little importance in itself, it is satisfactory to observe how well this date accords with the periods assigned by me from the Vaṃçāvalī for the adjacent reigns. See Table I.

Some difficulties, such as the date A.D. 1662, remarked on in the note to Table II., do no doubt occur even in comparatively recent times; yet on the other hand, as has been before pointed out, we find the tradition preserved, somewhat confusedly it is true, but still unmistakeably, of an interesting event like the establishment of the Çrīharsha era[1].

In the present work I have occasionally (as at pp. 8—9) ventured on a historical conjecture or tentative correction of the Vaṃçāvalī, which may be taken for what it is worth till further historical material comes to hand.

What the particular origin (*Herkunft*) of the Nepalese Vaṃçāvalī may be, I have no means of knowing, and should be glad to learn anything to supplement the statements of Dr Wright and Pandit Bhagvānlāl on the subject.

[1] See Wright pp. 131—2 and 134, cited in my Catalogue p. xli *et alibi*.

Dr Windisch, in the course of a courteous and detailed notice, thinks my description of the Mahāvastu too lengthy, because I "knew that it would be edited by M. Sénart." I was indeed aware that he had begun it, but as to when it may be finished I have no information.

I am indebted to the same reviewer for corrections of my reading of the colophon of Add. 1643 (pp. 151—2).

As to the last two corrections, the former, *sanāttanāṃm* (for p. 152, l. 5), I am afraid I do not fully understand. The latter, *samvatsare* for *samvatso*, is merely typographical and had appeared in the corrigenda of the catalogue, opposite page 1.

On page 178, l. 2, I must decline to accept Dr Windisch's *praṇāça* for *praṇala*. The verses in question deal with the supply of water, and in a well-irrigated country like Nepal the *praṇāli* or *praṇāla* (conduit) plays an important part. The word occurs in various forms both in Dr Bhagvānlāl's inscriptions and in those now published.

My friend Pandit Durgāprasāda of Jeypore, who manifested an interest that quite surprised me in a literature new to him, was good enough to read through a considerable part of my catalogue and favoured me with several emendations, which I have found on comparing them with the originals at Cambridge to be quite correct.

I have to thank all my critics for the appreciative way in which they have treated my palæographic essay; and it is some satisfaction to note that Professor Bühler, in his Appendix to Professor Max Müller's and Bunyiu Nanjio's "Ancient Palm-leaves from Japan" has followed precisely the same lines with frequent references to our earliest MSS.

On merely palæographic grounds I confess I was not at all surprised to find doubts expressed, like those of Professor Beal in the *Athenæum*, July 4th, 1885, as to the very early date assigned to those palm-leaves. The fact is that, as was pointed out in the review of Professor Max Müller's publication in the same journal for October 4th, 1884, the balance of archaism in forms of letters is, even on Professor Bühler's showing, rather in favour of the Cambridge MS., e.g. in the form of य.

I now subjoin the list of corrections that I have been able to make from these and other sources.

Page vi, line 6, for 1065, read 1039.

„ 29, „ 14, 15, for °चरणांङ्कधूलिध्वसराणां read °णाङ्-धूलिधू°.

Page 32, „ 8, for युङ्कुवन्ति read यंकुचन्ति [i. e. संकु°].

„ „ „ 11, for पदस्य read पादस्य.

„ 82, „ 14, 15, for पराङ्ड्रीं ... नितचाह्° read पराध्यीं .... मित°.

Page 93, last line, for Add. 1164 read Add. 1161.

„ 157, last line but one, for [सुपि] read [खि] and dele (sic).

„ 175, line 4, for 11—117 read 11—84, 84*, 85—117.

„ 182, „ 2, „ 1694 read 1691. 4.

Index, p. 210, col. 2. Add cross-reference: Laṅkāvatāra, see Saddharma-laṅkāvatāra.

P. 211, col. 1 } Under Saddharma-laṅkāv° add a reference to and 222, col. 2. } p. 20.

P. 212. Add a reference to Sarvajñamitra of Kashmir, p. 29.

P. 217, col. 1, line 10. For 104 read 106.

The use of *piṭaka* at p. 21, l. 3 seems also to merit insertion in Index III.

INDEX.

This index chiefly deals with the names of persons and of places visited. The titles of MSS. (not the names of their authors) are also included, and printed in italics, in cases where some special notice or citation is given in the text.

CAMBRIDGE: PRINTED BY C. J. CLAY, M.A. AND SON, AT THE UNIVERSITY PRESS.